Biography Today

Profiles of People of Interest to Young Readers

Author Series

Volume 12

Cherie D. Abbey
Managing Editor

Omnigraphics

615 Griswold Street • Detroit, Michigan 48226

Cherie D. Abbey, *Managing Editor*
Kevin Hillstrom and Laurie Hillstrom, *Staff Writers*
Barry Puckett, *Research Associate*
Allison A. Beckett and Linda Strand, *Research Assistants*

Omnigraphics, Inc.

* * *

Matthew P. Barbour, *Senior Vice President*
Kay Gill, *Vice President — Directories*
Kevin Hayes, *Operations Manager*
Leif Gruenberg, *Development Manager*
David P. Bianco, *Marketing Consultant*

* * *

Peter E. Ruffner, *Publisher*
Frederick G. Ruffner, Jr., *Chairman*

Copyright © 2002 Omnigraphics, Inc.
ISBN 0-7808-0610-7

The information in this publication was compiled from the sources cited and from other sources considered reliable. While every possible effort has been made to ensure reliability, the publisher will not assume liability for damages caused by inaccuracies in the data, and makes no warranty, express or implied, on the accuracy of the information contained herein.

This book is printed on acid-free paper meeting the ANSI Z39.48 Standard. The infinity symbol that appears above indicates that the paper in this book meets that standard.

Printed in the United States

Contents

Preface

Welcome to the twelfth volume of the **Biography Today Author Series**. We are publishing this series in response to suggestions from our readers, who want more coverage of more people in *Biography Today*. Several volumes, covering **Artists, Authors, Scientists and Inventors, Sports Figures, and World Leaders,** have appeared thus far in the Subject Series. Each of these hardcover volumes is 200 pages in length and covers approximately 10 individuals of interest to readers ages 9 and above. The length and format of the entries are like those found in the regular issues of *Biography Today*, but there is **no duplication** between the regular series and the special subject volumes.

The Plan of the Work

As with the regular issues of *Biography Today*, this special subject volume on **Authors** was especially created to appeal to young readers in a format they can enjoy reading and readily understand. Each volume contains alphabetically arranged sketches. Each entry provides at least one picture of the individual profiled, and bold-faced rubrics lead the reader to information on birth, youth, early memories, education, first jobs, marriage and family, career highlights, memorable experiences, hobbies, and honors and awards. Each of the entries ends with a list of easily accessible sources designed to lead the student to further reading on the individual and a current address. Obituary entries are also included, written to provide a perspective on the individual's entire career. Obituaries are clearly marked in both the table of contents and at the beginning of the entry.

Biographies are prepared by Omnigraphics editors after extensive research, utilizing the most current materials available. Those sources that are generally available to students appear in the list of further reading at the end of the sketch.

Indexes

A new index now appears in all *Biography Today* publications. In an effort to make the index easier to use, we have combined the **Name** and **General Index** into one, called the **Cumulative Index**. This new index contains the names of all individuals who have appeared in *Biography Today* since the series began. The names appear in bold faced type, followed by the issue in which they appeared. The Cumulative Index also contains the occupations, nationalities, and ethnic and minority origins of individuals profiled. The Cumulative Index is cumulative, including references to all individuals who have appeared in the *Biography Today* General Series and the *Biography Today* Special Subject volumes since the series began in 1992.

The Birthday Index and Places of Birth Index will continue to appear in all Special Subject volumes.

Our Advisors

This series was reviewed by an Advisory Board comprised of librarians, children's literature specialists, and reading instructors to ensure that the concept of this publication — to provide a readable and accessible biographical magazine for young readers — was on target. They evaluated the title as it developed, and their suggestions have proved invaluable. Any errors, however, are ours alone. We'd like to list the Advisory Board members, and to thank them for their efforts.

Sandra Arden, *Retired*
Assistant Director
Troy Public Library, Troy, MI

Gail Beaver
University of Michigan School of Information
Ann Arbor, MI

Marilyn Bethel, *Retired*
Broward County Public Library System
Fort Lauderdale, FL

Nancy Bryant
Brookside School Library,
Cranbrook Educational Community
Bloomfield Hills, MI

Cindy Cares
Southfield Public Library
Southfield, MI

Linda Carpino
Detroit Public Library
Detroit, MI

Carol Doll
Wayne State University Library and Information Science Program
Detroit, MI

Helen Gregory
Grosse Pointe Public Library
Grosse Pointe, MI

Jane Klasing, *Retired*
School Board of Broward County
Fort Lauderdale, FL

Marlene Lee
Broward County Public Library System
Fort Lauderdale, FL

Sylvia Mavrogenes
Miami-Dade Public Library System
Miami, FL

Carole J. McCollough
Detroit, MI

Rosemary Orlando
St. Clair Shores Public Library
St. Clair Shores, MI

Renee Schwartz
Broward County Public Library System
Fort Lauderdale, FL

Lee Sprince
Broward West Regional Library
Fort Lauderdale, FL

Susan Stewart, *Retired*
Birney Middle School Reading Laboratory, Southfield, MI

Ethel Stoloff, *Retired*
Birney Middle School Library
Southfield, MI

Our Advisory Board stressed to us that we should not shy away from controversial or unconventional people in our profiles, and we have tried to follow their advice. The Advisory Board also mentioned that the sketches might be useful in reluctant reader and adult literacy programs, and we would value any comments librarians might have about the suitability of our magazine for those purposes.

Your Comments Are Welcome

Our goal is to be accurate and up-to-date, to give young readers information they can learn from and enjoy. Now we want to know what you think. Take a look at this issue of *Biography Today*, on approval. Write or call me with your comments. We want to provide an excellent source of biographical information for young people. Let us know how you think we're doing.

Cherie Abbey
Managing Editor, *Biography Today*
Omnigraphics, Inc.
615 Griswold Street
Detroit, MI 48226
www.omnigraphics.com

An Na 1972-

Korean-Born American Novelist
Winner of the 2002 Michael L. Printz Award for *A Step from Heaven*

BIRTH

An Na was born on July 17, 1972, in South Korea. Her mother, An Jin Suk, is a chef. Her father, An Jung Young, is an engineer. She has one younger sister, An Jin, and one younger brother, An Sung.

An Na uses the Korean form of her name. In Korean names, the family name comes first, followed by the person's given name. So "An" is her family name, and "Na" is her given name, what Americans would call her first name.

———— " ————

"I remember reading books and falling under a spell, stepping into another world, becoming another person. More than television or movies, I could identify with the protagonist simply because she or he was not portrayed for me. While there might have been descriptive passages about what the character looked like, the beauty of a book stems from the way in which readers can overtake words. It's harder to do that in movies and television because the image is so present. Words have built in spaces for the readers to make themselves cozy."

———— " ————

YOUTH

An and her family moved from Korea to California when she was four years old. The prospect of living in the United States excited young An. But after she and her parents settled in San Diego, she found it very difficult to adjust to American life. She did not know how to speak or read English, and she was unfamiliar with the customs and culture of her new land. In addition, her Asian features set her apart from her mostly white classmates, and some of them mistreated her just because of her ethnic background.

As An grew older and gained an understanding of the English language, she took great comfort in books. They helped her understand the culture and history of the United States, and reading was an activity that provided her with peace and quiet. "I would read all the time," she recalled. "I used to lock myself in the bathroom for hours—since that was the only room with a lock—and read until my mom threatened to break down the door."

On many occasions, An would become so absorbed in a book's plot and characters that she would completely lose track of her surroundings. "I remember reading books and falling under a spell, stepping into another world, becoming another person," she said. "More than television or movies, I could identify with the protagonist simply because she or he was not portrayed for me. While there might have been descriptive passages about what the character looked like, the beauty of a book stems from the way in which readers can overtake words. It's harder to do that in movies and television because the image is so present. Words have built in spaces for the readers to make themselves cozy."

Despite her love of literature, however, An never thought about being a writer during her adolescence. "It wasn't a possibility to even think of it since creative fields are usually discouraged by [immigrant] parents," she explained. Instead, many immigrant parents want their children to concentrate on attaining professional careers in more traditional fields, like law, medicine, or academics.

An recalls many happy moments with friends and family in her youth. But she notes that "when I look back at my teenage years I can see two distinct personalities. There was the real me, which was gregarious, liked to laugh and have fun, who showed up at my Korean church, and then there was the school me, quiet, softspoken, hardly raised her hand in class. The two different sides related directly to my peers. . . . Only at my church, where all my friends were Korean, did I feel like I could be myself. Here, my peers understood and shared the same culture and issues that I dealt with at home and outside of church. My best friends growing up were Korean church friends."

EDUCATION

An attended classes in the San Diego public school system. "I was in all honors classes which consisted mostly of white students," she said. "I can only remember a few other people of color in my classes if at all. It had been that way since elementary school. I was quite shy and self-conscious in that environment, having been teased when I was younger for being different."

An graduated from Patrick Henry High School in 1990. She then enrolled at Amherst College in Amherst, Massachusetts. Four years later, she graduated magna cum laude with a Bachelor of Arts degree (BA) in Women's and Gender Studies. But it was a course in children's literature, taken during her last semester at Amherst, that set An on her future career path.

The children's literature class awakened new thoughts and desires in An. As she read and studied famous works written for young people, she began to entertain the possibility of writing for the first time. She then drew on her imagination to write a picture book story of her own. It was at that point that she realized that she loved writing. "I loved the process, the

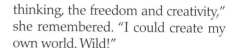

> *"[When] I look back at my teenage years I can see two distinct personalities. There was the real me, which was gregarious, liked to laugh and have fun, who showed up at my Korean church, and then there was the school me, quiet, softspoken, hardly raised her hand in class. The two different sides related directly to my peers. . . ."*

thinking, the freedom and creativity," she remembered. "I could create my own world. Wild!"

After graduating from Amherst in 1994, An began a career as a teacher of English and history. But she was also determined to explore further her newfound enthusiasm for writing and storytelling. So she decided to continue her education at Norwich University in Vermont. In 2000 she graduated from Norwich with a Master of Fine Arts degree (MFA) in writing children's literature.

CAREER HIGHLIGHTS

Finding Her Writing Voice

From 1994 to 2000, An taught English and history classes to middle school children. But during much of this period, she also took classes at Norwich University. It was while taking these classes that she found her voice as a writer. "Only after starting the MFA [Master of Fine Arts] program did I experience the realities of writing full time," she said. "All the elements that made writing so fantastic were still there, but along with the thrill was the discovery of the day-to-day process. Writing, revising, editing, rewriting, re-revising, cutting, chopping, crumbling, all of that was also writing. There are times when the words come to me as though spirited through the skies by writing fairies and there are times when I wander around my office picking lint off books."

An began writing *A Step from Heaven* as part of her course work at Norwich. This first novel was based on her own experiences growing up in California. "I started with one single impression from my childhood — the memory of my mother taking me to have my hair curled shortly after we arrived in California, since she realized that this was what most Americans looked like," she recalled. "And the story just took off from there as I added vignettes from my memory and was encouraged by people's positive response to what I was writing."

But even as the manuscript for *Step* grew in size, An became increasingly unhappy with it. "I realized at a certain point that my skills as a writer were not up to par with what I visualized and heard in my head," she explained. "I could not make the words that I was writing convey the emotions and sentiments that were in my mind. I had to put the book down and work on something else. I wrote an entire middle grade novel, that I eventually chucked, before going back to *Step*. . . . Finally, when I went back to *Step*, I was ready to do the hard work. And this time I knew I could do it."

By the time An earned her master's degree in children's literature in 2000, she had also completed her manuscript for *A Step from Heaven*. One of her academic advisors offered to show the book to an editor at a publishing house. To An's delight, the editor quickly offered to publish the novel, and one year later *A Step from Heaven* arrived on bookstore shelves all across America.

A Step from Heaven

A Step from Heaven explores issues of cultural identity, family ties, and adolescent self-image. This debut novel tells the story of a Korean-born girl named Young Ju who moves to the United States with her parents when she is five years old. Arranged by chapters that show Young Ju at various stages of adolescence, the book captures some of the most important and meaningful events in her life. In the early chapters of *A Step from Heaven*, the narrative shows Young Ju's difficult transition to her new life and surroundings. It then focuses on her struggle to balance two conflicting issues: her own desire to be accepted by other students as a fellow American, and her desire to comply with the demands of her parents, who insist that she speak Korean at home and follow traditional Korean ways. Finally, the novel depicts Young Ju's relationship with her father, a proud man who becomes so angry and disillusioned with disappointments in America that he turns into an abusive alcoholic.

"Only at my church, where all my friends were Korean, did I feel like I could be myself. Here, my peers understood and shared the same culture and issues that I dealt with at home and outside of church. My best friends growing up were Korean church friends."

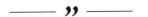

A Step from Heaven attracted a great deal of attention from readers and critics alike, and reviewers showered it with praise. Some critics emphasized An's skill at portraying Young Ju's emotional responses to her confusing and conflicted life. "This beautifully written book, a tale of both tragedy and eventual triumph, is likely to bring tears to the eyes of any reader," declared *Voice of Youth Advocates*. "Its author must be considered an important new voice in Asian-American children's literature." Others critics pointed out the author's wonderful storytelling instincts. For example, JadeMagazine.com observed that "the language of this book mirrors Young Ju's gradual acclimation into American society. *A Step from Heaven* is initially full of Korean words and broken English; however, as Young Ju's English improves Na also improves the quality of the book's sentence structure."

> *In writing* **A Step from Heaven,** *An Na says, "I started with one single impression from my childhood — the memory of my mother taking me to have my hair curled shortly after we arrived in California, since she realized that this was what most Americans looked like. And the story just took off from there as I added vignettes from my memory and was encouraged by people's positive response to what I was writing."*

Altogether, reviewers cited the book as a superb debut by an undeniably talented and insightful writer. *Booklist,* for example, described the novel as "a stirring immigration story [in which] the particulars of one Korean-American family speak to universal conflicts between home and outside. Each chapter is a story in itself, with dramatic surprise or quiet reversal. The tales blend together into a beautiful coming-of-age drama that will grab teens and make them think of their own conflicts." *School Library Journal* added that the book does a fine job of exploring the many difficulties faced by immigrants to America: "adjusting to strange customs, learning a new language, dealing with government bureaucracy, adults working two jobs each, and children embarrassed by their parents' behavior. Woven throughout is the underlying theme of dealing with an alcoholic and abusive father. Na has effectively evoked the horror and small joys of the girl's home life while creating sympathetic portraits of all the members of the family. A beautifully written, affecting work." *Multicultural Review,* meanwhile, declared that "[An's book] allows young people to step outside themselves for a moment and walk in the shoes of a hesitant, troubled peer who is not sure she likes being here [in America]. Poignant and powerful, the book is written with lyrical inventiveness that startles and delights and makes us see all things about us with new eyes."

———— " ————

"[A Step from Heaven]
grew from a need to
express some of the longings
and frustrations that
I felt as an immigrant
growing up in America.
Many people ask me if this
novel is autobiographical
and I always respond
by saying yes and no.
As with all writing,
the novel draws on
past emotions, but the
story is not my life.
What the protagonist
and I do share are some
of the feelings of yearning,
joy, and shame that
come with trying to
negotiate a foreign culture."

———— " ————

Finally, critics reserved special praise for An's depiction of the novel's young protagonist, who is a convincing blend of fragility and strength. "The book is endowed with a haunting grace by the exquisite voice of a new young writer," claimed the *New York Times Book Review*. "Young Ju is the emotional center of the book, and a wonderful character she is: feisty, observant, empathetic, and resourceful. As immigrant children do, she becomes an intermediary for her parents, translating America for them while trying, often unsuccessfully, to keep her American attitudes out of her home, where they land her in trouble. Her struggle to endure, and finally to rebel, makes a book full of heartbreaking scenes become, in the end, a story of triumph."

Drawing on Childhood Experiences

For her part, An felt that she accomplished her goal of making readers understand and appreciate the depth of Young Ju's struggles. "I wanted the reader to feel like they were reliving Young Ju's childhood with her," she explained. "Memory comes as a complete story with a beginning, middle, and end, [but it includes especially important moments] that focus on a smell or a touch or a feeling. This was what I wanted to convey when I began to construct Young Ju's life from a very young age to her years as a teenager. Hopefully, readers will leave the novel understanding how bits and pieces of Young Ju's childhood shaped who she became as an adult."

An freely admits that she drew heavily upon her own childhood experiences when she wrote *A Step from Heaven*. "[It] grew from a need to express some of the longings and frustrations that I felt as an immigrant growing up in America," she said. "Many people ask me if this novel is autobiographical and I always respond by saying yes and no. As with all writing, the novel draws on past emotions, but the story is not my life. What the protagonist and I do share are some of the feelings of yearning, joy, and shame that come with trying to negotiate a foreign culture."

An even acknowledges that some of the events that she describes in *A Step from Heaven* are based on childhood memories. But she stresses that "there are differences between Young's life and my own. The dynamics of her family were not the same as those of my own, yet I, too, felt that I couldn't be fully American given the expectations of my family, which was definitely a traditional Korean family. I drew upon that same experience of the duality of two cultures and the pull of trying to be a good daughter while absorbing the American ways I was learning at school."

Even though *A Step from Heaven* included fictional events, An admitted that she was not sure how members of her family would view the book. "I was initially afraid to show my father this book, because I knew that he would ask, 'Is this how you perceive me?'" she said. "But I didn't have to worry, because he got it exactly. He knew that my story was fictionalized, yet he said that he could see where it all came from. And my mother loved it. She is so proud of me that it is amazing. She can't stop toting the book to all my old schools."

Awards for the Novel

In the months following the publication of *A Step from Heaven*, the novel received a number of honors and awards. For example, it was selected as a finalist for the 2001 National Book Award, one of the greatest honors in American literature. But An did not even learn of this honor until days after the announcement. As it turns out, she and her husband were backpacking in Asia's Himalayan Mountains when the finalists were announced. Her editor sent her an e-mail message with the good news,

"There are differences between Young's life and my own. The dynamics of her family were not the same as those of my own, yet I, too, felt that I couldn't be fully American given the expectations of my family, which was definitely a traditional Korean family. I drew upon that same experience of the duality of two cultures and the pull of trying to be a good daughter while absorbing the American ways I was learning at school."

but he could do little else until An completed the hiking trip. "When James and I finally got out of the mountains, we had to travel through two villages before we could get Internet access," recalled An. "When we finally got through [and learned the news], James and I were jumping and whooping it up in this tiny Internet café. The whole experience has been kind of unbelievable. Nobody expects a first novel to get that much attention, let alone [get] nominated for such a prestigious award. Being at the awards ceremony felt like I had somehow crashed a party. Who let me in with all these amazing writers?"

"Writing is hard, but what other work lets you create a world and people of your own making? I have found no greater joy than stepping into a half complete story and asking my characters, 'What's next?' I could not imagine a better way to live."

Awards for *A Step from Heaven* continued to pile up in 2002. The most prestigious of these honors was the American Library Association's Michael L. Printz Award for excellence in literature for young adults. According to the chairperson of the Printz Award Selection Committee, An was a very deserving recipient: "Each chapter of [*A Step from Heaven*] is a stirring story, and together these lyrical vignettes create a heartfelt account of every teen's struggle between family and self."

An intends to be a writer for the rest of her life. In fact, she is hard at work on a second novel, about a relationship between a Korean-American girl and a Mexican-American boy. She admits that being a successful writer requires great motivation and discipline. "Trying to write five days out of the week as though it is a regular job is hard when there is no one else that you have to be accountable to except yourself," she explained. "Eventually for me, if I don't write, I get so antsy and guilt-ridden that I have to go and do the work." Indeed, An believes that her writing ability is a gift that she should take full advantage of. "Writing is hard, but what other work lets you create a world and people of your own making?" she said. "I have found no greater joy than stepping into a half complete story and asking my characters, 'What's next?' I could not imagine a better way to live."

HOME AND FAMILY

An married James F. Nagle, an educational consultant, in 1997. They divide their time between homes in Oakland, California, and Warren, Vermont. They are currently celebrating the birth of their first child, a girl.

An Na backpacking at Dzongri-la, a peak in Sikkim, India.

HOBBIES AND OTHER INTERESTS

An enjoys a wide variety of outdoor activities, including running, backpacking, and telemark skiing.

WRITINGS

A Step from Heaven, 2001

HONORS AND AWARDS

Best Book (*School Library Journal*): 2001
Best Children's Books (*Publishers Weekly*): 2001
Editor's Choice (*Booklist*): 2001
New York Times Book Review Notable Book: 2001
Best Book for Young Adults (American Library Association): 2002
Children's Book Award in Young Adult Fiction (International Reading Association): 2002
Dorothy Canfield Fisher Children's Book Award Master List: 2002
Fanfare Book (*Horn Book Magazine* Honor List): 2002
Michael L. Printz Award (American Library Association): 2002

Notable Books for a Global Society (International Reading Association): 2002

Notable Children's Book (American Library Association): 2002

FURTHER READING

Periodicals

Booklist, June 1, 2001, p.1881; Nov. 15, 2001, p.567; Jan. 1, 2002, p.766
New York Times Book Review, May 20, 2001, p.22
Publishers Weekly, Apr. 2, 2001, p.65; June 25, 2001, p.23; Feb. 4, 2002, p.22
School Library Journal, May 2001, p.156
USA Today, Mar. 5, 2002, p.D7

Online Articles

http://www.cynthialeitichsmith.com/auth-illAnNa.htm
   (*Cynthia Leitich Smith Children's Literature Resources,* "Interview with Young Adult Author An Na," Dec. 2001)
http://www.jademagazine.com/16ae_anna.html
   (*Jade Magazine,* "A Step in the Right Direction: Author An Na," Nov.-Dec. 2001)
http://www.teenreads.com/reviews/1886910588.asp
   (*TeenReads.com,* review of *A Step from Heaven,* undated)

Other

Additional information for this profile was obtained from private correspondence with An Na.

ADDRESS

Front Street
20 Battery Park Avenue
Asheville, NC 28801

WORLD WIDE WEB SITE

http://www.frontstreetbooks.com/all_writers.htm

Claude Brown 1937-2002

American Writer and Lecturer
Author of *Manchild in the Promised Land*

BIRTH

Claude Brown was born on February 23, 1937, in New York City. His father, Henry Lee Brown, worked in a railroad yard. His mother, Ossie Brock Brown, worked as a housekeeper and cleaning lady. Brown was the second of four children. He had one younger brother, nicknamed "Pimp," and two sisters, Carole and Margie.

YOUTH AND EDUCATION

Brown grew up in a poor, crime-ridden section of New York City called Harlem, which was composed almost entirely of African-Americans. His parents had moved to Harlem from South Carolina in 1935 in hopes of building a better life for themselves. But Harlem turned out to be a very difficult place in which to raise a family. The only home they could afford was a cramped apartment in an old building that was heavily scarred by graffiti and windblown trash. Crime and poverty riddled Harlem's streets, and the issues of alcohol and drug abuse were terrible problems in many homes.

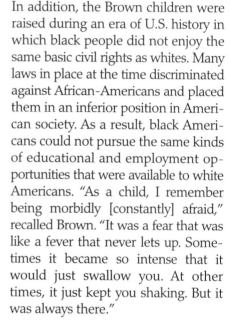

"As a child, I remember being morbidly afraid. It was a fever that never lets up. Sometimes it became so intense that it would just swallow you. At other times, it just kept you shaking. But it was always there.

In addition, the Brown children were raised during an era of U.S. history in which black people did not enjoy the same basic civil rights as whites. Many laws in place at the time discriminated against African-Americans and placed them in an inferior position in American society. As a result, black Americans could not pursue the same kinds of educational and employment opportunities that were available to white Americans. "As a child, I remember being morbidly [constantly] afraid," recalled Brown. "It was a fear that was like a fever that never lets up. Sometimes it became so intense that it would just swallow you. At other times, it just kept you shaking. But it was always there."

Alcoholism menaced the Brown family, too. Henry Lee Brown was a heavy drinker, and when he became drunk he sometimes behaved violently toward members of his family. On some occasions he hauled young Claude with him to Harlem's dark and dingy bars, where his son would watch him get drunk with other men from the neighborhood. But Claude was also a frequent target of his father's anger, and he recalled that his father often "pounded" him for his poor performance in school or for not listening to him. "I really didn't care, because I was just waiting and wondering — waiting till I got big enough to kick his ass and wondering if he would want to talk then," Brown remembered.

Brown's childhood was a troubled one almost from the very beginning. By the time he reached school age, young Claude — known as "Sonny" to his friends—was spending nearly all of his time out on Harlem's crime-infested streets. He soon learned to fight and steal and talk tough, and he became acquainted with the neighborhood's leading drug dealers and gang leaders. By age nine he was an official member of a street gang called the Harlem Buccaneers, and a proud recruit in the gang's special "Forty Thieves" division of burglars and thieves. Years later, Brown recalled that he treasured his membership in the Buccaneers because of the friendships he forged with some fellow members. In addition, being part of a well-known street gang gave him "a sort of social status" within Harlem that he enjoyed.

By age 10, Brown rarely bothered to attend school. When he did show up, he seemed to spend more time stealing or fighting than reading class assignments. Brown's truancy and his disruptive behavior led the school to expel him on several occasions. These expulsions enraged his father, who administered several angry beatings as punishment for his behavior. But the beatings only pushed him farther away from his family and deeper into criminal activity.

By 1947, Brown's behavior had become so uncontrollable that his family and legal authorities agreed on a plan to send him to South Carolina to live on his grandparents' farm for a year. They hoped that by removing him from Harlem's crime-infested streets, he might settle down and develop an interest in school. To his surprise, Brown found that he enjoyed the quiet pace of rural life. He became accustomed to the routine of farm chores, and he liked living in a place where he did not have to worry about his safety. But when he returned to Harlem one year later, he resumed his illegal activities as if he had never been gone.

Criminal Activity Leads to Reform School

At age 11, Brown was arrested for breaking into a store. A judge ordered him to attend the Wiltwyck Reformatory, a facility for emotionally disturbed and deprived boys. Brown spent the next two years at Wiltwyck, which placed a strong emphasis on discipline and order. In some ways, this environment did not seem to have much of an impact on the troubled youth. For example, he stole money and possessions from staff members and other students alike. But during these two years at Wiltwyck, he also developed a relationship with Dr. Ernest Papanek, the school director and psychologist. Brown recognized that Papanek genuinely cared about the boys in the school, and he later called him "probably the smartest and the deepest cat I had ever met." Over time, Brown and the doctor established a bond that continued well into Brown's adult life.

Despite Papanek's positive influence, Brown fell back into his old self-destructive ways when he was released from Wiltwyck at age 13. He returned to Harlem, where he began using and selling marijuana on the street. He also engaged in a wide assortment of other criminal activities, from burglary and mugging to violent clashes with members of other street gangs. On one occasion, he was even shot in the stomach while attempting to steal some bedsheets from a clothesline.

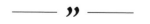

In reform school, Brown started reading biographies of celebrities and historical figures and learned how these famous people had triumphed over racism, poverty, and other challenges. Soon he began to assess his own future. "I started getting ideas about life. I wanted to know things and I wanted to do things. It made me start thinking about what might happen if I got out of Warwick Reformatory and didn't go back to Harlem."

The bullet wound actually increased Brown's stature among his fellow gang members. But the shooting also confirmed his belief that his old Harlem neighborhood had become even more deadly and menacing during the two years he spent at Wiltwyck. He blamed this deterioration on the increased popularity of heroin, a highly addictive drug. Brown avoided heroin after one nasty experiment with it, but many other people in Harlem —including his brother and some of his friends—were being destroyed by the drug. "It was a bad time," Brown later wrote. "It was a bad time for me because I was sick. I was sick of being at home. I was sick of the new Harlem, the Harlem I didn't know, the Harlem I couldn't find my place in."

Building a Better Life

At age 14, Brown was sent to New York's Warwick Reformatory for nine months. During his stay there, he was befriended by Mrs. Cohen, the wife of the school's superintendent. She recognized that a sensitive and curious mind lurked underneath Brown's anger and swagger. With this in mind, she convinced him to read biographies of celebrities and historical figures, from the white inventor Albert Einstein to black baseball player Jackie Robinson, who was the first African-American to play major league baseball. "She was the nicest lady I ever met," Brown recalled. "She was a real person."

Claude Brown (right) is pictured in this detail from the back cover of the original 1965 book jacket of Manchild in the Promised Land.

Through his reading, Brown learned about the ways in which these famous people had triumphed over racism, poverty, and other challenges to build successful lives for themselves. Soon he began to assess his own future. "I started getting ideas about life," he said. "I wanted to know things and I wanted to do things. It made me start thinking about what might happen if I got out of Warwick and didn't go back to Harlem."

Brown eventually completed three terms at Warwick before obtaining his final release in July 1953. He returned to Harlem, where he resumed his old activities as a drug dealer and thief. But he found that he no longer liked his old street life, and his thoughts increasingly turned to building a life for himself that would not involve drugs or burglary. Brown's unhappiness became even more intense when an addict robbed him of some drugs that he was carrying. Brown knew that he would have to kill the addict in order to preserve his street reputation as a tough guy, but the thought of killing another human being filled him with sadness. A short time later, the addict was arrested by police, sparing him from making a decision about whether to commit murder. But the incident helped convince Brown that he needed to steer his life into another direction.

A short time later, Brown made the dramatic decision to return to school. The 16-year-old signed up for a series of night courses at Washington Irving High School in Manhattan. Over the next few years, he attended classes regularly, ignoring the taunts of old friends who still passed their days dealing drugs on street corners. During this time, he supported himself by working as a busboy, deliveryman, shipping clerk, bookkeeper, and postal clerk. After several months he moved into an apartment in a vibrant area of New York City called Greenwich Village. He soon befriended a group of village-area jazz musicians, and within a matter of months he was spending hours at a time practicing jazz arrangements on the piano.

Between the demands of work, school, and piano practice, Brown had little time for partying or fooling around. But he loved the new life he had made for himself because "for the first time in ages, I felt as though I was really doing things. . . . I felt I was a grown man, and I had to go out and make my own life. This was what the moving was all about, growing up and moving out on my own." Brown also loved the sense of freedom that he felt in Greenwich Village. "I gave my gun away when I moved out of Harlem," he explained. "I didn't need any kind of protection because I wasn't afraid anymore. I had been afraid in Harlem all my life."

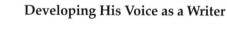

> "[For] the first time in ages, I felt as though I was really doing things," Brown said about his new life in Greenwich Village. "I felt I was a grown man, and I had to go out and make my own life. This was what the moving was all about, growing up and moving out on my own."

Developing His Voice as a Writer

After graduating from Irving Washington High School in 1957, Brown returned to his old Harlem neighborhood. He found that many of his childhood companions were dead, in prison, or hopelessly addicted to drugs. Determined to avoid a similar fate, he decided to continue his education. In 1959 he used a financial grant from a New York City church to enroll at Howard University in Washington, D.C. Brown studied government and business at Howard, but he also took a number of writing classes (one of his instructors was Toni Morrison, who later became a famous novelist). In the early 1960s he published several articles on urban and African-American issues for national magazines.

Brown graduated from Howard with a bachelor's degree in 1965. He then briefly attended law school at Stanford University in California and concluded his formal schooling by taking several classes at Rutgers University in New Jersey.

CAREER HIGHLIGHTS

Brown wrote only two books in his lifetime, but one of them—*Manchild in the Promised Land*—was among the most famous works published in America during the 20th century. In *Manchild,* Brown told the world about his grim childhood and his eventual escape from a life of drugs and crime. In the process, he educated readers about the awful conditions in which many urban African-American lived. In addition, his book revealed the deep feelings of anger and hopelessness that dominated many African-American neighborhoods across the country. As a result, *Manchild* was credited with helping readers understand how these emotions boiled over in both positive and negative ways in the 1960s. During this period, black anger and pride sparked the emergence of a civil rights movement that eventually forced the United States to remove many unfair laws that discriminated against African-Americans. But feelings of helplessness and rage also fueled destructive race riots that ruined many inner city areas in the late 1960s.

Brown loved the sense of freedom that he felt in Greenwich Village. "I gave my gun away when I moved out of Harlem. I didn't need any kind of protection because I wasn't afraid anymore. I had been afraid in Harlem all my life."

Deciding to Write About His Childhood

In the early 1960s Brown was approached by his old friend and counselor Dr. Papanek. Papanek asked the young writer to consider writing an article on Harlem for *Dissent,* a national magazine. Brown agreed, and when his article was published several months later, the Macmillan Publishing Company offered him a $2,000 advance to write an entire book about growing up in Harlem.

Brown embraced the idea, and in 1963 he began working on the book. He worked on it for the next two years. By the time he finished, he had written 1,537 pages, and he delivered it to the publisher in a grocery box. The manuscript sat unread at the Macmillan offices for a year before it was assigned to a new editor, Alan Rinzler. So Brown, Rinzler, and other editors at Macmillan began the difficult process of editing his autobiography down to a more manageable size. "He had an authentic voice—violent, funny, and optimistic," Rinzler later said. Finally, in 1965, *Manchild in the Promised Land* was published.

The cover from the 1965 edition of Manchild in the Promised Land.

In the opening pages of *Manchild,* Brown explained that he decided to write about his troubled youth. He wanted to show America the sense of despera-tion and hopelessness that was engulfing so many African-American children in Harlem and elsewhere. He related many of those problems to a monumental change that occurred in American society beginning in the late 1800s — the migration of many Southern blacks to the cities of the North.

"I want to talk about the first Northern urban generation of Negroes. I want to talk about the experiences of a misplaced generation of a misplaced people in an extremely complex, confused society. This is a story of their searching, their dreams, their sorrows, their small and futile rebellions, and their endless battle to establish their own place in America's greatest metropolis — and in America itself.

The characters are sons and daughters of former Southern sharecroppers. These were the poorest people of the South, who poured into New York City during the decade following the Great Depression. These migrants were told that unlimited opportunities for prosperity existed in New York and that there was no 'color problem' there. They were told that Negroes lived in houses with bathrooms, electricity, running water, and indoor toilets. To them this was the 'promised land' that Mammy had been singing about in the cotton fields for many years. . . .

[They] had neglected to tell the folks down home about one of the most important aspects of the promised land: it was a slum ghetto. There was a tremendous difference in the way life was lived up North. There were too many people full of hate and bitterness crowded into a dirty, stinky, uncared-for closet-size section of a great city. . . .

The children of these disillusioned colored pioneers inherited the total lot of their parents — the disappointments, the anger. To add to their misery, they had little hope of deliverance. For where does one run to when he's already in the promised land?"

Response to the Book

Manchild in the Promised Land caused an immediate sensation. It became a national bestseller, and critics across the country praised Brown for his searing descriptions of the terrible problems that urban African-Americans faced every day. William Mathes, writing in the *Antioch Review*, added that "I began *Manchild* reluctantly and came to weep and laugh over it, finishing with mounting excitement. . . . I was profoundly moved. . . . More than any book I have read in years, *Manchild* probes past the fabric of order and conventional response and finds that place in all of us that knows about pain and terror and the slim hope of being born by chance and dead for sure."

—— **"** ——

*"[Manchild] is written
with brutal and unvarnished
honesty in the plain talk of
the people, in language that
is fierce, uproarious, obscene,
and tender, but always
sensible and direct. . . .
Claude Brown speaks for
himself — and the Harlem
people to whom his life is
bound — with open dignity,
and the effect is both
shattering and deeply satisfying." — Romulus Linney,*
**New York Times
Book Review**

—— **"** ——

Similar ideas were voiced by Romu-lus Linney, writing in the *New York Times Book Review*. Linney wrote that *Manchild* "is written with brutal and unvarnished honesty in the plain talk of the people, in language that is fierce, uproarious, obscene, and ten-der, but always sensible and direct. . . . Claude Brown speaks for himself — and the Harlem people to whom his life is bound — with open dignity, and the effect is both shattering and deeply satisfying. . . . The final strength of this autobiography rests in the sur-vival of the author himself. How did it come about? . . . His book reveals that his personal regeneration [re-birth] came not only from dedicated individuals and institutions, not only from his own toughness and clarity of mind, but from the agonies of the de-feated friends he so deeply respected and loved, who have been destroyed."

Brown appreciated the kind words, and he was delighted that the book became a bestseller. But the respon-ses to the book that he most treasured came from other young African-American men who had grown up in similar circumstances. "I would get letters from brothers who were stationed in Vietnam, who were from places that I didn't think had blacks. They would write things like, 'Hey brother, are you sure your father didn't have a twin, because he sure sounds like mine.' And some would say, 'Thanks for writing our story.' I re-alized after reading some of these letters, this wasn't just my biography. It was the biography of an entire generation of African-Americans."

Speaking Out on African-American Issues

By the late 1960s, *Manchild in the Promised Land* had transformed Brown into one of America's best-known commentators on African-American urban life. He regularly appeared on television and radio programs to dis-cuss issues of importance to African-Americans, and he testified before special Congressional committees on crime. He made a number of controversial statements during his testimony that further heightened his public profile. For example, he repeatedly urged legislators to legalize drugs, saying that it would reduce crime in the inner city.

Brown briefly explored a career in teaching, leading a creative writing class at the University of California-Santa Barbara in the summer of 1969. But he was soon spending most of his time writing and lecturing on African-American issues. In 1976 Brown completed and published *The Children of Ham,* a book about a group of orphaned and runaway children who forge a loose "family" together in an abandoned building in Harlem.

Some reviewers praised *The Children of Ham* as a worthy sequel to *Manchild.* The reviewer Chris Smith wrote in *Best Sellers* that "Brown as a writer has once again magnificently portrayed the poetry of human existence. The reader laughs, weeps, and lives with the children of Ham. Highly recommended." But the book was not a commercial success, and other reviewers felt that it did not pack the same emotional power as *Manchild.* Some critics even questioned the authenticity of Brown's story. "If the book were well written, perhaps it would not matter whether it was true or not," asserted Anatole Broyard in the *New York Times.* "But Mr. Brown cannot write at all. . . . It is a toss-up who is more boring—Mr. Brown, in his sententious [pompous or self-important] social worker's jargon, or the 'children' themselves."

In the 1980s Brown spent a lot of time in Harlem and other urban areas, studying how the lives of inner-city African-Americans and other poor people were changing. During his travels, he expressed amazement at the rise in violent crime committed by teens and the casual attitude of some

———— " ————

Brown treasured the responses to **Manchild** *that came from other young black men who had grown up in similar circumstances. "I would get letters from brothers who were stationed in Vietnam, who were from places that I didn't think had blacks. They would write things like, 'Hey brother, are you sure your father didn't have a twin, because he sure sounds like mine.' And some would say, 'Thanks for writing our story.' I realized after reading some of these letters, this wasn't just my biography. It was the biography of an entire generation of African-Americans."*

———— " ————

Brown testifies before a Senate committee on slum life in the ghetto, August 1966.

young men about taking the life of another human being. He also felt great sorrow about Harlem's continued slide deeper into violence and poverty. In one 1984 article written for the *New York Times,* he claimed that Harlem had become a symbol of all American urban areas where drugs, violence, and poverty had smothered the community's sense of opportunity, hope, and pride.

In 1987 Brown hosted a special television program called "Manchild Revisited: A Commentary by Claude Brown." The show, which appeared on national public television, discussed crime in American cities and possible ways of curbing illegal activity. During the course of the special, Brown offered his own views on the issue. He declared his support for capital punishment and decriminalization of drugs, and urged cities to launch programs to raise the quality of police departments. In addition, "Manchild Revisited" visited housing projects in Cleveland and Washington where crime rates had dropped dramatically after residents organized neighborhood patrols. "'Manchild Revisited' doesn't make a case for vigilantism [punishing criminals despite a lack of legal authority] but for volunteerism, especially among poor blacks," commented the *New York Times*. "As a woman in Washington says, 'the residents have to take charge of their community.' . . . 'Manchild Revisited' is an intelligent examination of an enormously important issue."

In the 1990s Brown started a third book comparing his childhood experiences in Harlem with a history of Harlem in the 1980s, when crack cocaine became a terrible problem. But he was unable to finish the project, and he spent his last years lecturing on African-American issues to a wide variety of audiences, from college students to troubled youth. He also worked in a mentoring program in Harlem that helped students go to college, and he actively supported programs for troubled youths in Newark, New Jersey, where he lived the last quarter-century of his life. Brown died of a lung ailment on February 2, 2002.

———— " ————

"Manchild in the Promised Land chronicled [Brown's] ascent from a harrowing childhood of violent crime and poverty in Harlem and became a classic of American literature. Published at the heights of the civil rights movement, the book reached far beyond the traditional literary world, drawing new attention to the lives of urban blacks. . . . The heart of the book to many was its evocation of an astonishing culture of violence that gripped Harlem's poor children almost from birth."
—*Robert F. Worth,* New York Times

———— " ————

Claude Brown's Legacy

Today, Brown's literary reputation clearly rests on *Manchild in the Promised Land*, which is now considered an American classic. To date, the book has sold more than four million copies and has been translated into 14 languages. It continues to sell 30,000 copies each year, and it is still required

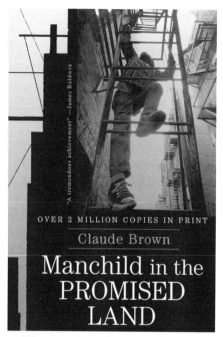

The cover from the 1999 edition of
Manchild in the Promised Land.

"

Manchild in the Promised Land *has had a far-reaching influence that continues to this day. "It was just groundbreaking in so many ways," said Mark Gompertz from Simon and Schuster. "No one had written with such honesty and vivid detail. It had a raw, gritty type of writing. He was an original voice."*

"

reading in many high school and college classes. Written with a direct style sprinkled liberally with profanity, *Manchild* shocked readers with its graphic and vivid depictions of violence, drug dealing, prostitution, and other realities of ghetto life. It opened up a new world for many readers and drew attention to the lives of many African-Americans. "*Manchild in the Promised Land* chronicled [Brown's] ascent from a harrowing childhood of violent crime and poverty in Harlem and became a classic of American literature," Robert F. Worth wrote in the *New York Times*. "Published at the heights of the civil rights movement, the book reached far beyond the traditional literary world, drawing new attention to the lives of urban blacks. . . . The heart of the book to many was its evocation of an astonishing culture of violence that gripped Harlem's poor children almost from birth."

Manchild in the Promised Land has had a far-reaching influence that continues to this day. "It was just groundbreaking in so many ways," said Mark Gompertz from Simon and Schuster (the company that now owns the book's original publisher, Macmillan). "No one had written with such honesty and vivid detail. It had a raw, gritty type of writing. He was an original voice."

MARRIAGE AND FAMILY

Brown married Helen Jones on September 9, 1961. They had two children, but their marriage ended in divorce. His companion during the last years of his life was Laura Higgins.

WRITINGS

Manchild in the Promised Land, 1965
The Children of Ham, 1976

Brown also contributed articles to *Esquire, Life, Los Angeles Times*, the *New York Times*, and other periodicals.

HONORS AND AWARDS

Anisfield-Wolf Book Award: 1966, for furthering race relations

FURTHER READING

Books

Adams, A. John, and Joan Martin Burke. *Civil Rights: A Current Guide to the People, Organizations, and Events,* 1970
Applegate, Edd. *Literary Journalism: A Biographical Dictionary of Writers and Editors,* 1996
African-American Almanac, 1994
Authors and Artists for Young Adults, Vol. 7, 1991
Contemporary Authors, Vol. 73-76, 1978
Contemporary Authors, New Revision Series, Vol. 81, 1999
Oxford Companion to African American Literature, 1997
Schomburg Center Guide to Black Literature From the Eighteenth Century to the Present, 1996

Periodicals

Antioch Review, Fall 1965, p.456
Best Sellers, Sep. 1976, p.207
Black Issues Book Review, May-June 2002, p.80
Black Issues in Higher Education, Feb. 28, 2002, p.26
Chronicle of Higher Education, Apr. 12, 2002, p.5
Current Biography Yearbook, 1967, 2002
Harper's, May 1985, p.39
Jet, Feb. 25, 2002, p.55

Los Angeles Times, May 17, 1988, Metro section, p.7; Mar. 24, 1994, p.B7; Feb. 7, 2002, p.B14

New Republic, May 8, 1976, p.25

New York Post, July 18, 1965, p.39

New York Magazine, Jan. 30, 1989, p.35

New York Times, Apr. 16, 1976, p.25; Feb. 10, 1987, p.C18; Feb. 6, 2002, p.B8; Feb. 10, 2002, p.L4

New York Times Book Review, Aug. 22, 1965, p.1

New York Times Magazine, Sep. 16, 1984, p.36; Apr. 14, 1996, p.6

Washington Post, Feb. 7, 2002, p.B7

Online Articles

http://www.anisfieldwolf.org/newsarticle.cfm?articleID=597&PTSidebarO ptID=128&returnTo=page471.cfm&returntoname=Winners&SiteID=29 (*Anisfield-Wolf Book Awards,* undated)

http://www.cjcj.org/centennial/brown.html (*Justice Policy Institute,* "Second Chances/Claude Brown,"undated)

Online Database

Biography Resource Center, 2002, article reproduced from *Contemporary Authors Online*

Meg Cabot 1967-

American Author of Young Adult Fiction and
Historical Romances
Author of *The Princess Diaries*

BIRTH

Meggin Patricia Cabot was born on February 1, 1967, in
Bloomington, Indiana. Her parents were A. Victor Cabot, a
college professor and researcher, and Barbara Cabot. She has
two brothers, Matthew and Nicholas.

YOUTH

Cabot was an imaginative child who enjoyed drawing, reading, and keeping a diary. One of her favorite summertime destinations was the Monroe County Public Library, which provided an air conditioned refuge from the heat. She loved to pluck books from the library's shelves and curl up in a nice, cool corner of the room.

As an adolescent, however, Cabot was not particularly fond of novels written specifically for YA (young adult) audiences. "Even when I was a kid, I never really read YA!" she admitted. "I mean, I read the *Chronicles of Narnia,* and some Judy Blume, but that's about it. I was a huge sci-fi fan, and that is all I read back then."

> *"I was pretty much a huge geek," Cabot says about high school. She was also preoccupied with boys. "Most of what's in my journals from those days is about boys, boys, boys, and that's why I am the only one who is allowed to look at them! It is too embarrassing!"*

EDUCATION

Cabot received her elementary and high school education in Bloomington. Cabot claims that by the time she reached high school, "I was pretty much a huge geek." Like many teen girls, she was also preoccupied with boys. "Most of what's in my journals from those days is about boys, boys, boys, and that's why I am the only one who is allowed to look at them! It is too embarrassing!"

In terms of class subjects, Cabot developed a strong dislike for mathematics during her high school years. "I actually flunked algebra, like the main character in my [*Princess Diaries*] books . . . so that was my least favorite subject. Even though I loved to write, I never liked English lit. class very much. I think it ruins books when you dissect them too much. I liked my art classes best." Cabot's favorite extracurricular activity, meanwhile, was drama. "In high school, I wanted to be an actress," she recalled. "Until I got to college and took some creative writing courses. Then I decided I wanted to become a novelist."

Cabot studied creative writing at Indiana University, which is based in her hometown of Bloomington. But art continued to interest her as well, and she earned her Bachelor of Fine Art degree (BFA) when she graduated in 1991.

CAREER HIGHLIGHTS

Meg Cabot is best known as the author of *The Princess Diaries,* a funny series of books about a self-conscious, awkward American teenager who learns that she is a member of another country's royal family. In 2001, the first book of the series was made into a hit movie starring Anne Hathaway and Julie Andrews. But Cabot has written a wide range of other popular books for teen and adult audiences as well, from supernatural YA thrillers like the *Mediator* and *1-800-WHERE-R-YOU* series to historical romances like *Kiss the Bride.* In these books, which have been published under Cabot's name as well as several pseudonyms, the author has displayed a knack for creating entertaining, imaginative storylines and capturing the hopes, dreams, fears, and attitudes of adolescent girls.

Turning a Hobby into a Career

After graduating from Indiana, Cabot moved to New York City to pursue a career as a freelance illustrator. She accepted a position as assistant manager of an undergraduate dormitory at New York University, then began looking for opportunities to display her drawing talent. As time passed, however, she found herself spending more of her free time writing romance stories than hunting down work as an illustrator. Writing stories "was my hobby," Cabot explained. "After a while, I had so many romances on my hard drive, it was getting ridiculous. Everybody I knew kept saying to me, 'Why don't you try to get published?' But I loved writing so much that I was afraid if I sent one of my novels to a publisher and it was rejected, I would be crushed, and I would eventually grow to hate my beloved hobby."

But the death of Cabot's father in 1994 changed her attitude about writing. "When someone you love dies, it puts things in perspective," she said. "I realized you only have a limited amount of time on this planet, and if you spend it sitting around being afraid of rejection, you will never know what you could have accomplished, if you'd just tried. So about a week after my dad's funeral, I sent my first manuscript out to a publisher. And it was promptly rejected."

After enduring a series of rejections from publishers, Cabot decided to find a literary agent to help her find a home for one of her romantic novels. She sent letters to more than two dozen agents, only to have all but one of them reject her request for representation. But one agent agreed to sign Cabot up as a client. One year later, the agent sold Cabot's first book, a historical romance for adults called *Where Roses Grow Wild,* which she had written under the pseudonym Patricia Cabot.

After *When Roses Go Wild* was published in 1998, Cabot found it much easier to sell other adult romances. From 1998 to 2001, she wrote six historical romances — romantic novels set in earlier historical eras like 19th-century England — that she published under the name of Patricia Cabot. These works were praised by readers and reviewers alike for their fresh and entertaining plots, interesting characters, and steamy relationships. "Cabot writes romance almost without peer," commented *Publishers Weekly,* "creating passionate love scenes readers will swoon over, delivered with poetry and beauty, and memorable secondary characters."

> ———— " ————
>
> *"Almost everything in my* [Princess Diaries] *books has happened to me at one time or another. I was never a princess, but when I was in high school I had a crush on an older boy — lots of them actually — who didn't seem to know I was alive. I had a bossy best friend and I flunked algebra, several times, oh my mum was dating and is now living with one of my teachers. It was and still is excruciating!"*
>
> ———— " ————

The Princess Diaries

Despite the popularity of her romance novels, however, Cabot found even greater success as a writer of books for young adults. Her best-known work in this genre to date is *The Princess Diaries*, a 2000 bestseller that became a summer box office success with the Disney film one year later. According to Cabot, she based *The Princess Diaries* on events in her own life. "I was inspired to write *The Princess Diaries* when my mom, after the death of my father, began dating one of my teachers, just as Mia's mom does in the book!" she explained. "I have always had a 'thing' for princesses (my parents used to joke that when I was little, I did a lot of insisting that my 'real' parents, the king and queen, were going to come get me soon, and that everyone had better start being a LOT nicer to me) so I stuck a princess in the book just for kicks." Finally, Cabot drew from her own high school diary entries in writing the book, which is told in diary format.

The Princess Diaries is told from the perspective of 14-year-old Mia Thermopolis, a nice but insecure teen. Her life is turned upside down when she learns that she is actually the princess of a small country called Genovia. As the book unfolds, Mia grapples not only with her stern "grandmere"

(grandmother), who wants to turn her into a proper princess, but also with a blizzard of problems that almost every teenage girl faces, from difficult homework to crushes on handsome boys. "Almost everything in my [*Princess Diaries*] books has happened to me at one time or another," said Cabot. "I was never a princess, but when I was in high school I had a crush on an older boy—lots of them actually—who didn't seem to know I was alive. I had a bossy best friend and I flunked algebra, several times, oh my mum was dating and is now living with one of my teachers. It was and still is excruciating!"

The Princess Diaries caused quite a stir when it was published. *School Library Journal* claimed that "readers will relate to Mia's bubbly, chatty voice and enjoy the humor of this unlikely fairy tale. . . . This funny, fast-paced book should appeal to hip young women, including reluctant readers." *Booklist* added that *The Princess Diaries* was a "hilarious story" that is "like reading a note from your best friend."

Shortly after *The Princess Diaries* hit bookstore shelves, the Walt Disney Film Company paid Cabot for the right to make a film based on her story. "I was VERY excited when I found out Disney would be making a movie from my book," remembered Cabot. "And I thought [director] Garry

Marshall did a great job — and that Anne Hathaway made the perfect Mia. At first I was a little iffy when I heard Julie Andrews would be playing Grandmere — Julie is too nice to play such a mean character! But when I saw Julie's performance, I knew she had just the right amount of regalness mixed with grandmotherly warmth. . . . I saw the finished film for the first time at the premiere in [Los Angeles in 2001]. I think I laughed harder than anybody else in the entire audience. It was a hoot to see my characters on the screen."

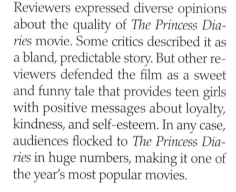

"I hope girls will realize that they are not alone in feeling the way I did when I was in high school — like a great big freak! Also that 'normal' is not what they see on TV. Being true to yourself and to your friends, is way more important than being part of the 'in crowd.' . . . . We all need to take a deep breath and remember it's what's inside that counts."

Reviewers expressed diverse opinions about the quality of *The Princess Diaries* movie. Some critics described it as a bland, predictable story. But other reviewers defended the film as a sweet and funny tale that provides teen girls with positive messages about loyalty, kindness, and self-esteem. In any case, audiences flocked to *The Princess Diaries* in huge numbers, making it one of the year's most popular movies.

In 2001 Cabot published a sequel about Mia's adventures called *Princess Diaries II: Princess in the Spotlight*. Fans of the first book in the series rushed to scoop up the novel, which carried the author's trademark blend of teen fantasy and high school drama. "The plot careens along with outrageous characters doing outrageous things, but in the context of the story, 'outrageous' seems quite normal," observed *School Library Journal*. In 2002, a third installment in the *Princess Diaries* series — *Princess in Love* — was released. Once again, Cabot uses Mia's diary as a storytelling device to tell readers all about her struggles with teen social life and the demands of being a princess. "When some of [Mia's] greatest dilemmas are discovering the nuances of French kissing and a one-day suspension for thwarting a student walkout, readers can't help but love this self-obsessed (i.e., normal) teenager," said *School Library Journal*.

Cabot loves the Mia character, and she has indicated that she plans to write many more stories about the unlikely teen princess over the next several years. "I would like to follow Mia through all four years of high school," she said. "Considering each book takes place during a two-week period of time, this is going to make for a lot of books!" Cabot also believes that she can continue to balance the escapist fantasy elements of the series with helpful hints about surviving high school with a sense of humor and a strong sense of self-worth. "I hope girls will realize that they are not alone in feeling the way I did when I was in high school — like a great big freak!" said Cabot. "Also that 'normal' is not what they see on TV. Being true to yourself and to your friends, is way more important than being part of the 'in crowd.' . . . . We all need to take a deep breath and remember it's what's inside that counts."

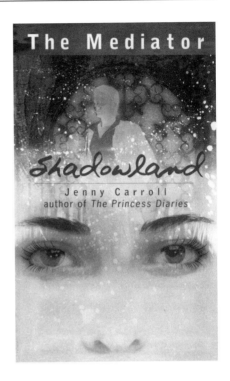

Writing Supernatural Tales Under the Name Jenny Carroll

Lifted by the great success of her *Princess Diaries,* Cabot has also launched two other book series for young adults. Both of these YA series — *Mediator* and *1-800-WHERE-R-YOU* — feature teen girls as their main characters. But unlike the stories about Mia, Cabot incorporated strong elements of mystery and the supernatural into these new series.

Cabot unveiled the *Mediator* and *1-800-WHERE-R-YOU* series in 2000 under the pen name Jenny Carroll. When asked why she chose to write other YA novels under a different name, Cabot explained that the new series were written for both male and female audiences. "I have far more male fans for my works written as Jenny Carroll than for my works written under my real name," she confirmed.

The action in Cabot's *Mediator* stories centers around a California teenager named Suze who has the ability to see and communicate with ghosts. To date, there are four books in the series: *Shadowland* (2000), *Ninth Key* (2001), *Reunion* (2001), and *Darkest Hour* (2001). In each book, Suze tries to bring peace to restless spirits, but these efforts place her life in jeopardy. At the same time, Suze deals with boy trouble, family problems, and other challenges that confront countless other teens.

Cabot uses her home state of Indiana as the setting for the *1-800-WHERE-R-YOU* books: *When Lightening Strikes* (2001), *Code Name Cassandra* (2001), *Safe House* (2002), and *Sanctuary* (2002). In the first book in this series, *When Lightning Strikes*, readers are introduced to 16-year-old Jessica, who gains psychic powers after being struck by lightning. She wants to use her strange new abilities to find missing children, but government agents want to use her for their own purposes. Reviewers hailed *When Lightning Strikes* as a promising first installment. "Jessica's thrilling first-person account of her adventure is enhanced by raucously funny teen observations," stated *Booklist*. "Colorful characters, multilayered conflict, and biting wit jumpstart the *1-800-WHERE-R-YOU* series at high speed."

> "I think it's important for all teens — not just girls — to feel empowered. Adolescence is a crummy thing to go through, and a lot of kids feel isolated, or like freaks. I know I did. I just want to get the message out that if you feel like a freak, you are not alone: we all felt like freaks, and even these girls in my books, who are so strong and have so much going for them, feel left out sometimes. But guess what? You get over it."

In subsequent volumes in the series, Jess is torn between using her strange powers to help unfortunate families and her desire to be left alone. In *Code Name Cassandra,* for example, Jess's work as a counselor at a summer camp for musically gifted kids is thrown into turmoil when a grief-stricken father asks for help in finding his missing child. As with other YA novels written by Cabot, critics pointed to the believability of the teen characters in *Cassandra* as one of its strongest points. "With her detention-clouded past and her ambitionless future, [Jess] is no role model," admitted *School Library Journal*. "But she is a character that young people will believe and enjoy. The story moves fast and is full of suspense, action, and teen intrigue."

For her part, Cabot says that she gets a kick out of writing about Suze and Jessica and their strange abilities. "Everybody loves a good ghost story!" declared Cabot. "I just try to provide my readers with a different slant on the subject. And I have always wished that I had ESP, so the *1-800* books are kind of fantasy fulfillment for me."

Creating the "All-American Girl"

Cabot has published numerous books in the last few years. But despite her success with *The Princess Diaries* and other series, she continues to explore new story ideas. In 2002, for example, she wrote *All-American Girl,* about a teenage girl named Samantha Madison who becomes famous when she saves the president from an assassination attempt. "I think every kid— and some of us grown-ups, too— fantasizes about being a hero," said Cabot. "And what would be the most heroic thing of all? Saving the life of the most important man in the country, that's what! And that's what Samantha Madison does in *All-American Girl*

—though of course she is ANYTHING but the all-American girl. Being a national heroine is a bit of a burden for her." Cabot is also excited that Disney decided to buy the rights to make a film based on the *All-American Girl* story even before the book was published.

Recently, Cabot has been working on a series of historical romances for young adult readers. The first of these efforts, the 2002 romance *Nicola and the Viscount,* features a 16-year-old orphan named Nicola Sparks who is growing up in the high society setting of early 19th-century England. As the novel begins, she is certain that a fellow named Lord Sebastian should be her future husband. But as time passes, doubts about Sebastian's character take root at the same time that she develops an interest in Nathaniel, her best friend's brother. Cabot has also been exploring the idea of writing stories exclusively in electronic format, and she has agreed to release *The Princess Diaries* and some other earlier works in electronic form. In addition, in fall 2002 she published her first adult contemporary novel, *The Boy Next Door,* written under the name Meggin Cabot.

ON WRITING FOR TEENS

Cabot is amused by people who express surprise at her ability to write convincingly about teen issues and attitudes. "[They] always want to know,

———— " ————

"I write what I write because it gives me pleasure. If I had no writing contracts or movie deals, I would still write exactly the kind of stories I am writing right now. The fact that these stories are being published, and that people are paying money to read them, is an inexpressible joy to me. It does not trouble me that none of my books are likely to win Pulitzers. . . . To do what you love is what life is all about, and to be paid for it . . . well, what could be better than that?"

———— " ————

'How do you know so much about teenagers? You don't have any kids," she related. "Well, the fact is, I was a teenager once, and I remember what it was like, in all of its angst-ridden horror. Also, I worked for 10 years in a freshman dormitory at New York University. If that doesn't put you in touch with the teen psyche, I don't know what will."

Cabot believes that her realistic portrayals of teen issues are a big reason why her titles are so popular. "[*The Princess Diaries*] really does reflect modern day popular culture, as well as modern-day teen problems and concerns," she claims. "I try to make sure that my books for young readers, though they may be about princesses or girls who can talk to ghosts, also portray the realities that teens cope with on a daily basis."

Still, Cabot admits that she only likes to feature certain types of teens as her main characters. "I don't want to read stories about wimps, so I don't write stories about them," she said. "I think it's important for all teens — not just girls — to feel empowered. Adolescence is a crummy thing to go through, and a lot of kids feel isolated, or like freaks. I know I did. I just want to get the message out that if you feel like a freak, you are not alone: we all felt like freaks, and even these girls in my books, who are so strong and have so much going for them, feel left out sometimes. But guess what? You get over it."

Cabot is working hard to nurture her blossoming writing career. She admits that she usually doesn't begin her day until nine a.m. or so. But once she is up she usually writes all day until her husband comes home from work, stopping only for lunch and occasional work outs. And when she's "on a roll," she says that she'll work until well after midnight. In addition, she sometimes undertakes long hours of research for her writing projects, even though she dislikes this aspect of the book creation process. This is especially true for her adult romance titles, since fans of this writing genre are "real sticklers for historical accuracy." Cabot remembers one occasion when she spent hours and hours looking up information on 19th-century pistols for one of her adult books. "Basically, I had to do all that research for something that appears in maybe one sentence of dialogue," she said. "But if you are not trying to the best of your ability to remain within the confines of historical accuracy in your historical fiction, what is the point?"

With this philosophy in mind, Cabot urges teens and other people interested in writing to work hard and prepare themselves for disappointment. After all, few writers become successful after only a few months of work. "I have thousands (literally) of rejections to show for my efforts," stated Cabot. "In fact, when I speak at schools now about the writing experience, I try to bring my enormous USPS [U.S. Postal Service] mail bag of rejection letters with me, to share with the kids what being a writer seems sometimes to *really* be about: sticking to it even when it seems like no one in the entire world wants to read your stuff."

But Cabot persevered, and she is now one of the best-known writers of YA novels in America. "I write what I write because it gives me pleasure," she said. "If I had no writing contracts or movie deals, I would still write exactly the kind of stories I am writing right now. The fact that these stories are being published, and that people are paying money to read them, is an inexpressible joy to me. It does not trouble me that none of my books are likely to win Pulitzers. . . . To do what you love is what life is all about, and to be paid for it . . . well, what could be better than that?"

MARRIAGE AND FAMILY

Cabot married Benjamin D. Egnatz, a financial market writer, on April 1, 1993. They live in Greenwich Village, a neighborhood in New York City. They have no children.

WRITINGS

Young Adult Fiction Written as Meg Cabot

The Princess Diaries, 2000
The Princess Diaries II: Princess in the Spotlight, 2001
The Princess Diaries III: Princess in Love, 2002
All-American Girl, 2002
Nicola and the Viscount, 2002

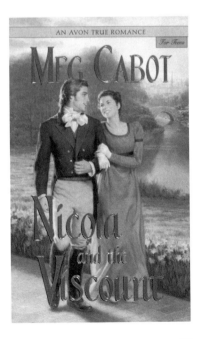

Young Adult Fiction Written as Jenny Carroll

***The Mediator* Series**
Shadowland, 2000
Ninth Key, 2001
Reunion, 2001
Darkest Hour, 2001

1-800-WHERE-R-YOU Series
When Lightning Strikes, 2001
Code Name Cassandra, 2001
Safe House, 2002
Sanctuary, 2002

Adult Historical Romances Written as Patricia Cabot

Where Roses Grow Wild, 1998
Portrait of My Heart, 1998
An Improper Proposal, 1999
A Little Scandal, 1999
Lady of Skye, 2001
Educating Caroline, 2001
Kiss the Bride, 2002

Adult Contemporary Novel Written as Meggin Cabot

The Boy Next Door, 2002

HONORS AND AWARDS

Best British Isles Historical Romance (*Romantic Times*): 1999, for *An Improper Proposal*
Top Ten Quick Picks for Reluctant Readers (American Library Association): 2001, for *The Princess Diaries*
Best Book Selection (American Library Association): 2001, for *The Princess Diaries*
Teen Book for the New Millennium (New York Public Library): 2001, for *The Princess Diaries*

FURTHER READING

Periodicals

Booklist, May 15, 2001, p.1744; Jan. 1, 2002, p.841
Boston Herald, July 27, 2001, p.29

Daily Variety, Aug. 30, 2001, p.1
Entertainment Weekly, Aug. 10, 2001, p.49
Indianapolis Star, Jan. 3, 2001, p.G6
Kirkus Reviews, Apr. 1, 2002, p.488
New York Times, Aug. 3, 2001, p.E11
Publishers Weekly, Oct. 9, 2000, p.88; Nov. 6, 2000, p.92; July 9, 2001, p.21;
    Apr. 22, 2002, p.56
School Library Journal, Oct. 2000, p.155; Aug. 2001, p.176; Jan. 2002, p.131;
    Apr. 2002, p.142
Toronto Sun, Jan. 6, 2002, p.S24
USA Today, Aug. 2, 2001, p.D4

Online Articles

http://www.bbc.co.uk/schools/communities/onionstreet/comms/megtr
    script.shtml (*Onion Street — BBC,* "Meg Cabot Interview," Dec. 11, 2001)
http://www.childrensexpress.org/dynamic/public/the_princess_101201.htm
    (*Children's Express,* "The Princess Diarist," Dec. 10, 2001)
http://www.knowbetter.com/ebook/columns/detail.asp?id=69
    (*KnowBetter.com,* "Q and A with Princess Diaries Author Meg Cabot,"
    Mar. 22, 2002)
http://www.likesbooks.com/cabot.html
    (*All About Romance Web Site,* "Patricia Cabot: Cross-Genre
    Phenomenon," July 23, 2001)
http://www.readersread.com/features/megcabot.htm
    (*ReadersRead.com,* "Interview with Meg Cabot," undated)
http://www.theromancereader.com/cabot.html
    (*The Romance Reader,* "Meet Author Patricia Cabot," May 16, 2001)

ADDRESS

HarperCollins Children's Books
1350 Avenue of the Americas
New York, NY 10019

WORLD WIDE WEB SITES

http://www.megcabot.com (*Meg Cabot Home Page*)
http://www.patriciacabot.com (*Patricia Cabot Home Page*)
http://www.jennycarroll.com (*Jenny Carroll Home Page*)

Virginia Hamilton 1936-2002

American Writer for Children and Young Adults
Newbery Medal-Winning Author of Stories about the
African-American Experience

(Editor's Note: In 1995, Biography Today *featured Virginia Hamilton in* Biography Today Author Series, *its first special volume devoted solely to writers of interest to young readers. Since that time, she published several additional works that further burnished her reputation as one of the world's finest writers of books for young adults. Hamilton's death in 2002 was mourned not only by her*

friends and family, but also by countless loyal readers and fellow writers throughout the world. For these reasons, Biography Today *has decided to provide readers with a special retrospective essay that details her professional accomplishments in her last years and commemorates the matchless contributions she made to children's literature over the course of her long career. For detailed information on her childhood, education, and career up to 1995, please see our original profile in* Biography Today Author Series, Volume One.)

CAREER HIGHLIGHTS

By the mid-1990s, Virginia Esther Hamilton had become one of the literary world's most respected authors of books for children and young adults. Moreover, she was acknowledged as one of America's most talented chroniclers of the African-American experience. Indeed, she could look back with pride on a string of critically acclaimed novels that had garnered some of literature's greatest honors, including the Newbery Medal, the National Book Award, and the *Boston Globe-Horn Book* Award. The finest of these works—*Zeely* (1967), the *Dies Drier Chronicles* (1968 and 1987), *The Planet of Junior Brown* (1971), *M.C. Higgins, the Great* (1974), *The People Could Fly: American Black Folktales* (1985), *Anthony Burns* (1988), *Cousins* (1990), and *Many Thousand Gone: African Americans from Slavery to Freedom* (1992)—were already widely regarded as classics of children's literature. "If her ability to create subtle impressions with a few simple strokes is exceptional, even more extraordinary is Ms. Hamilton's use of language," commented the *New York Times Book Review*. "Like the gift of perfect pitch, she has an ear for the cadences of everyday conversations and internal debates. She re-creates the language of African-American children in prose as smooth and liquid as poetry."

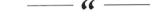

"If her ability to create subtle impressions with a few simple strokes is exceptional, even more extraordinary is Ms. Hamilton's use of language. Like the gift of perfect pitch, she has an ear for the cadences of everyday conversations and internal debates. She re-creates the language of African-American children in prose as smooth and liquid as poetry." —New York Times Book Review

In 1992 Hamilton was awarded the Hans Christian Anderson Medal, one of the most prestigious international awards in children's literature. But this honor, which paid tribute to her long and distinguished writing career,

Some of Hamilton's Acclaimed Early Works

1967

1968

1971

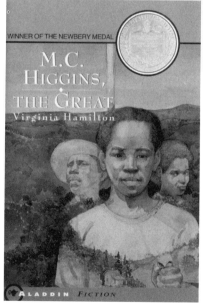

1974

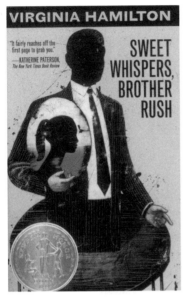

1982

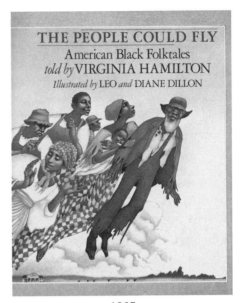

1985

1988

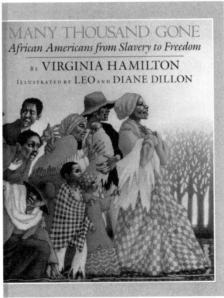

1992

Hamilton's early works won many medals and awards. In 1992 she was awarded the Hans Christian Andersen Medal, and in 1995 she earned the Laura Ingalls Wilder Medal. These prestigious awards paid tribute to her long and distinguished writing career and her contribution to children's literature.

53

did not cause her to relax or cut back on her writing in any way. She continued to devote her life to writing, a life-long passion that had sprouted from her rural childhood in Ohio, where she had been raised in a loving family full of gifted storytellers. "I write books because I love chasing after a good story and seeing fantastic characters rise out of the mist of my imaginings," she explained. "I can't explain how it is I keep having new ideas. But one book inevitably follows another. It is my way of exploring the known, the remembered, and the imagined, the literary triad of which all stories are made."

"I write books because I love chasing after a good story and seeing fantastic characters rise out of the mist of my imaginings. I can't explain how it is I keep having new ideas. But one book inevitably follows another. It is my way of exploring the known, the remembered, and the imagined, the literary triad of which all stories are made."

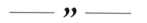

Exploring Ancient Folktales and Legends

In the mid-1990s Hamilton issued a number of books based on legends and folktales that had been passed down from generation to generation. In 1995 she published *Her Stories: African American Folktales, Fairy Tales, and True Tales,* a collection of legends and true stories about women of all ages, from small children to grandmothers. The book, which featured illustrations by Leo and Diane Dillon, was warmly received by critics. "Virginia Hamilton and the Dillons have produced yet another superb offering, of value to all ages and segments of our society," stated *School Library Journal.* "Funny, touching, scary, magical, and inspiring. . . . Entrancing and important."

That same year, Hamilton released *When Birds Could Talk and Bats Could Sing: The Adventures of Bruh Sparrow, Sis Wren, and Their Friends.* In this fanciful collection, Hamilton retells old legends about birds and bats, including one that claims that bats were once the world's greatest singers until various birds stole all their best songs. As with other folktale collections retold by Hamilton, *When Birds Could Talk* could never have been made were it not for the author's research abilities. "One of the things that is highly unusual in Virginia's work is that she has been able to combine master storytelling and a remarkable ear for spoken language with scholarly research," confirmed Bonnie Verburg, who served as Hamilton's editor for more than 15

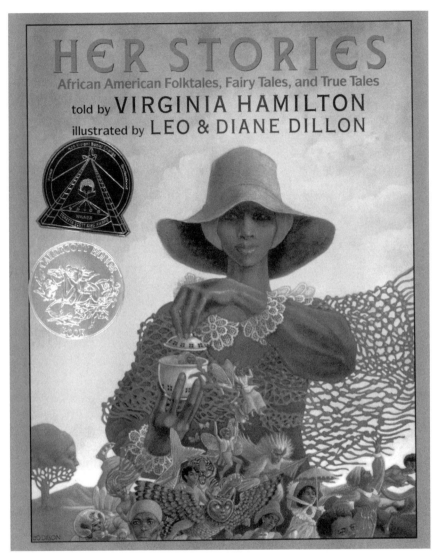

1995

years. "So you have this magnificent researcher who at the same time has a great ear for dialogue and the spoken word. She was able to find stories that had been buried and disappeared since the Civil War. She would dig them out, and what excitement when she found them!"

Hamilton continued to mine old animal legends for stories in the 1997 collection *A Ring of Tricksters: Animal Tales from America, the West Indies, and Africa.* In this book, illustrated by Barry Moser, the author gathered togeth-

Some of Hamilton's Acclaimed Later Works

1995

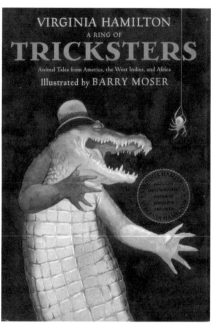

1997

1998

1999

er 11 stories based on old slave tales about sly and devious creatures of the animal world. *Kirkus Reviews* praised the volume as "a consummate collection . . . combining witty prose with breathtaking watercolors."

Hamilton greatly enjoyed retelling old legends and myths that had first been told in black communities back in the 18th and 19th centuries. But she also loved to create and tell stories about modern black life and the challenges of being a young person—black or white—in America. In the late 1990s Hamilton returned to these themes with *Second Cousins*, published in 1998. This book, which features the character Cammy from the author's 1990 classic young adult novel *Cousins*, uses a family reunion to examine issues of friendship, loyalty, and family bonds. In 1999 Hamilton published *Bluish*, a novel about two classmates who develop a deep friendship with a wheelchair-bound girl who suffers from leukemia (an often fatal disease). "The compelling writing and themes of friendship, compassion, and understanding make this title a must for every school and public library," declared *Voice of Youth Advocates.*

> "*Woven into her books is a deep concern with memory, tradition, and generational legacy, especially as they helped define the lives of American blacks from the days of slavery onward.*"
> —Margalit Fox,
> **New York Times**

Hamilton had built a well-deserved reputation for tackling difficult or unsettling issues in her writing. But she enjoyed immersing herself in playful, offbeat tales as well. Her taste for this type of story was on full display in *The Girl Who Spun Gold*, a 2000 picture book based on a West Indian version of the Rumplestiltskin fairy tale. One year later, she published a children's novel called *Wee Winnie Witch's Skinny: An Original Scare Tale for Halloween.*

Another 2001 book project to which Hamilton devoted a lot of her time was a young adult novel called *Time Pieces: The Book of Times*. This work is notable because it is a semi-autobiographical novel about an Ohio girl whose perspective on life changes after she hears how her grandfather escaped from slavery via the Underground Railroad, which parallels the experiences of Hamilton's ancestors.

Sadly, Hamilton passed away before this story based on her own childhood could be published. She died of breast cancer in Dayton, Ohio, on

February 19, 2002. But the author was able to complete the novel in her last months of life, and *Time Pieces: The Book of Times* is scheduled to be published in the fall of 2002.

HAMILTON'S LEGACY

———— " ————

Hamilton left an important legacy for readers of all ages and ethnic backgrounds. "It was Hamilton who showed me that with great writing, the more particular, the more universal," explained Hazel Rochman in Booklist. *"Rooted in her place, in her family, in American black history and culture, her stories speak to all of us. . . . Hamilton died on February 19. But her books will always speak to 'our most secret fearful heart.' Her words make us fly."*

———— " ————

Virginia Hamilton's death is a tremendous loss for the world of children's literature. In the days following her passing, writers from all over the globe offered testimonials about the enduring impact and quality of her novels and story collections. "She helped to launch the modern era of African-American children's literature, and from there, she went on to become one of America's premier writers of children's literature," observed Rudine Sims Bishop, professor of children's literature at Ohio State University. "She set the standard for quality in children's literature. . . . Her contributions were international. She won every award there is to win."

The testimonials honoring Hamilton's life and work touched on many different aspects of her writing. *The Guardian,* a newspaper in London, England, pointed out that "from the beginning, her stories were very different from the gritty realism of many of her contemporaries; they were not problem novels exploring deprived inner-city childhoods. Instead, they were stories of insight and imagination, rural as much as urban." The *Dayton Daily News*, meanwhile, highlighted the fact that "Hamilton's books took seriously the readers' abilities to understand. She didn't insult their intelligence by explaining what was important, she let the story do the work, unfolding in ways that grabbed the imagination, heart, and mind." Writing in the *New York Times*, Margalit Fox stressed the value of Hamilton's works in documenting and explaining the black American experience:

2000

"Woven into her books is a deep concern with memory, tradition, and generational legacy, especially as they helped define the lives of American blacks from the days of slavery onward."

But as numerous obituaries and appreciations noted, Hamilton left an important legacy for readers of all ages and ethnic backgrounds. "It was Hamilton who showed me that with great writing, the more particular, the more universal," explained Hazel Rochman in *Booklist*. "Rooted in her place, in her family, in American black history and culture, her stories speak to all of us. . . . Hamilton died on February 19. But her books will always speak to 'our most secret fearful heart.' Her words make us fly."

"Virginia Hamilton wrote 35 books for children, drawing on black history, mythology, memory, and idioms and beliefs for the stories which she shockingly described (at the time) as liberation literature," stated the *Herald,* a newspaper based in Glasgow, Scotland. "Her aim was to show her black characters' experience as different but integral to the American experience." And as many testimonials noted, Hamilton's rich legacy of literature was built on the foundation of her memories of her childhood and rich family history. As the *Herald* concluded, "American children and children throughout the rest of the world are fortunate that she shared [those memories] so intelligently and generously."

MARRIAGE AND FAMILY

Virginia Hamilton is survived by her husband Arnold Adoff, their son, Jaime Levi Adoff, and their daughter, Leigh Hamilton Adoff.

WRITINGS

Zeely, 1967
The House of Dies Drear, 1968
The Time-Ago Tales of Jahdu, 1969
The Planet of Junior Brown, 1971
W.E.B. Du Bois: A Biography, 1972
Time-Ago Lost: More Tales of Jahdu, 1973
Paul Robeson: The Life and Times of a Free Black Man, 1974
M.C. Higgins, the Great, 1974
The Writings of W.E.B. Du Bois, 1975 (editor)
Arilla Sun Down, 1976
Justice and Her Brothers, 1978 (first novel in the "Justice" trilogy)
Dustland, 1980 (second novel in the "Justice" trilogy)
Jahdu, 1980
The Gathering, 1981 (third novel in the "Justice" trilogy)
Sweet Whispers, Brother Rush, 1982
The Magical Adventures of Pretty Pearl, 1983
Willie Bea and the Time the Martians Landed, 1983
A Little Love, 1984
Junius over Far, 1985
The People Could Fly: American Black Folktales, 1985
The Mystery of Drear House: The Conclusion of the Dies Drear Chronicle, 1987
A White Romance, 1987
In the Beginning: Creation Stories from around the World, 1988
Anthony Burns: The Defeat and Triumph of a Fugitive Slave, 1988
Bells of Christmas, 1989
Cousins, 1990
The Dark Way: Stories from the Spirit World, 1990
The All Jahdu Storybook, 1991
Many Thousand Gone: African Americans from Slavery to Freedom, 1992
Drylongso, 1992
Plain City, 1993
Jaguarundi, 1994

Her Stories: African American Folktales, Fairy Tales, and True Tales, 1995
*When Birds Could Talk and Bats Could Sing: The Adventures of Bruh Sparrow,
    Sis Wren, and Their Friends,* 1995
A Ring of Tricksters: Animal Tales from America, the West Indies, and Africa,
    1997
Second Cousins, 1998
Justice and Her Brothers, 1998
Dustland, 1998
The Gathering, 1998
Bluish: A Novel, 1999
The Girl Who Spun Gold, 2000
Wee Winnie Witch's Skinny: An Original Scare Tale for Halloween, 2001
Time Pieces: The Book of Times, 2002

HONORS AND AWARDS

Notable Children's Books (American Library Association): 1967, for *Zeely;*
    1968, for *The House of Dies Drear;* 1974, for *M.C. Higgins, the Great;* 1976,
    for *Arilla Sun Down;* 1980-81, for the *Justice* trilogy; 1982, for *Sweet
    Whispers, Brother Rush;* 1983, for *The Magical Adventures of Pretty Pearl;*
    1983, for *Willie Bea and the Time the Martians Landed;* 1985, for *The People
    Could Fly;* 1988, for *Anthony Burns;* 1990, for *Cousins;* 1996, for *Her
    Stories: African American Folktales, Fairy Tales, and True Tales;* 1997, for
    When Birds Could Talk and Bats Could Sing
Edgar Allan Poe Award: 1969, for *The House of Dies Drear,* for best juvenile
    mystery
Lewis Carroll Shelf Award: 1971, for *The Planet of Junior Brown;* 1974, for
    M.C. Higgins, the Great; 1988, for *Anthony Burns*
Boston Globe — Horn Book Award: 1974, for *M.C. Higgins, the Great;* 1983,
    for *Sweet Whispers, Brother Rush;* 1988, for *Anthony Burns*
John Newbery Medal (American Library Association): 1975, for *M.C.
    Higgins, the Great*
National Book Award: 1975, for *M.C. Higgins, the Great*
Best Book for Young Adults (American Library Association): 1982, for
    Sweet Whispers, Brother Rush; 1988, for *Anthony Burns*
Coretta Scott King Award (American Library Association): 1983, for *Sweet
    Whispers, Brother Rush;* 1984, for *A Little Love;* 1989, for *Anthony Burns;*
    1996, for *Her Stories: African American Folktales, Fairy Tales, and True Tales*
New York Times Best Illustrated Children's Book Award: 1986, for *The People
    Could Fly*
Regina Medal (Catholic Library Association): 1990

Hans Christian Andersen Author Award (International Board on Books for Young People): 1992

Laura Ingalls Wilder Medal (American Library Association): 1995, honoring an author or illustrator whose books have made a substantial and lasting contribution to literature for children

MacArthur Fellowship Award (John D. and Catherine T. MacArthur Foundation): 1995

FURTHER READING

Books

Authors and Artists for Young Adults, Vol. 2, 1989; Vol. 21, 1997

Gallo, Donald R. *Speaking for Ourselves, Too: More Autobiographical Sketches by Notable Authors of Books for Young Adults,* 1993

Hipple, Ted, ed. *Writers for Young Adults,* Vol. 2, 1997

Jones, Lynda, and Ron Garnett. *Five Famous Writers,* 2001

Mikkelsen, Nina. *Virginia Hamilton,* 1994

Montreville, Doris de, and Elizabeth D. Crawford. *Fourth Book of Junior Authors and Illustrators,* 1978

Notable Black American Women, 1992

The 100 Most Popular Young Adult Authors, 1999

Something About the Author, Vol. 56, 1990, Vol. 79

St. James Guide to Young Adult Writers, 1999

Twentieth-Century Children's Writers, 1989

Wheeler, Jill C. *Virginia Hamilton,* 1997

Who's Who Among African Americans, 2001

Who's Who in America, 2002

Periodicals

Booklist, Mar. 15, 2002, p.1249

Columbus Dispatch, Feb. 21, 2002, p.E6

Dayton (Ohio) Daily News, Feb. 24, 2002, p.E1

Guardian (London), Mar. 1, 2002, p.26

Herald (Glasgow), Mar. 7, 2002, p.18

Horn Book, Dec. 1974; Aug. 1975, p.337; Sep.-Oct. 2002, p.631

Independent (London), Mar. 6, 2002, p.6

Los Angeles Times, Feb. 23, 2002, Metro, p.16

New York Times, Feb. 20, 2002, p.A19

New York Times Book Review, Nov. 11, 1990, p.34

School Library Journal, Apr. 2002, p.20

USA Today, Feb. 20, 2002, p.B9

Online Articles

http://www2.scholastic.com/teachers/authorsandbooks/authorstudies/
authorstudies.jhtml (*Scholastic*, "Author Studies Homepage," 2002)
http://teacher.scholastic.com/writewit/diary/descriptive_meet.htm
(*Scholastic*, "Descriptive Writing with Virginia Hamilton," 2002)

Online Database

Biography Resource Center, 2002, articles reproduced from *Authors and Artists for Young Adults,* 1997; *Contemporary Authors Online,* 2002; *Contemporary Black Biography,* 1995; *Notable Black American Women,* 1992; and *St. James Guide to Young Adult Writers,* 1999

WORLD WIDE WEB SITE

http://www.virginiahamilton.com

RETROSPECTIVE

Chuck Jones 1912-2002

American Cartoon Director and Animator
Pioneering Director of Warner Brothers' Cartoons
Featuring Bugs Bunny and Daffy Duck
Creator of the Road Runner and Wile E. Coyote
Cartoon Characters

BIRTH

Charles Martin (Chuck) Jones was born on September 21, 1912, in Spokane, Washington. He was the third of six children born to Charles Adams Jones and Mabel Martin Jones.

YOUTH

Throughout Jones's childhood, he and his family led a nomadic existence. Charles Jones uprooted his family time and again in order to pursue business schemes that he thought would make him rich. But each of these ventures ended badly: they either ended in failure or provided barely enough income for Jones to feed and clothe his family.

After years of wandering, the family finally settled down in southern California, where Charles Jones tried to make a living as an expert on avocados and as a geranium farmer. When the latter pursuit failed, he sold his farm to an interested buyer. Years later, Chuck Jones learned that the land upon which his father had planted geraniums had held rich deposits of crude oil that could have made the family very wealthy.

Chuck Jones grew up in a series of rental homes. As a result, he never developed any strong affection for a single house or neighborhood. But his father usually selected rental units that were near the Pacific Ocean, where young Chuck loved to play. In addition, Charles Jones always sought out homes that were already furnished with books as well as tables, chairs, and beds. An avid reader, the elder Jones encouraged his children to read in order to learn about the world around them. He wanted them to soak up everything—from the classics of literature to the backs of cereal boxes. "I read at four years of age, but lagged behind my sister who read at three," recalled Jones. "My father liked children, but didn't want to amuse them. He figured the best way to get us out of his hair was to teach us to read."

"I read at four years of age, but lagged behind my sister who read at three. My father liked children, but didn't want to amuse them. He figured the best way to get us out of his hair was to teach us to read."

Young Chuck Jones soon became fascinated with such books as Mark Twain's *Tom Sawyer* and *Huckleberry Finn*. He felt that the characters contained in the pages of those books were so believable that they were almost real. Jones also enjoyed Twain's *Roughing It*, a book about the American West that included descriptions of the coyote as a starving, desperate, luckless, yet determined creature. Years later, Jones would draw upon Twain's description of the animal in creating Wile E. Coyote, one of his most famous animated characters.

Jones also learned that unique and entertaining animal characters existed in the real world. When he was seven years old, his family adopted a stray cat that they named Johnson. The cat was unlike most other members of its species. For one thing, it actually enjoyed swimming in the ocean. But Johnson's most peculiar trait was its habit of eating grapefruit a half at a time and then wearing the empty rind on its head like a space helmet. Jones later credited his relationship with this unusual pet as an important factor in his successful career as an animator. "If there were personality differences [in cats]," Jones stated, "I was unaware of them until Johnson padded in on little fog feet and taught me that first and more important lesson of animation: individuality. Yes, in looking back, I can see that it all began with Johnson, because Johnson demonstrated with such vivid certainty the whole truth of the matter: it is the individual, the oddity, the peculiarity that counts."

Young Jones was also fascinated by motion pictures, which seemed to increase in popularity with each passing year. Indeed, he loved going to the movies as a youngster. He especially enjoyed watching films starring Charlie Chaplin, Buster Keaton, and the other great comedians of the silent-film era. But what Jones loved to do more than anything was draw pictures. In fact, his passion for drawing became stronger each year. At first, his father encouraged him and praised the quality of his efforts. As time passed, though, Charles Jones became convinced that his son would never be able to build a career out of his drawing abilities. "My father and I didn't get along very well," Jones once said, "because success meant everything to him. So we had a falling out."

EDUCATION

Jones attended many different schools in countless communities across the western United States. As he grew older, his performance at school declined significantly. Bored with most school subjects, he received average and even failing grades in many of his classes. Jones's indifference to his schoolwork eventually made his father so angry that he pulled him out of high school and sent him to the Chouinard Art Institute (later the California Institute of the Arts).

Jones welcomed the change, in part because it signaled that his father recognized that art might be his only path to success. "He figured I couldn't do anything else," Jones remarked. "And he figured if I went to art school I'd become famous." As it turned out, the young cartoonist thrived at Chouinard, earning his diploma in 1930.

"Rabbit Fire," 1951

CAREER HIGHLIGHTS

Chuck Jones ranks as one of the world's most famous animators of all time. He not only created beloved cartoon characters like Road Runner and Wile E. Coyote, he also produced some of the most legendary cartoon adventures for characters ranging from Bugs Bunny to Daffy Duck. He even helped bring Dr. Seuss's famed *How the Grinch Stole Christmas* to film. In recognition of his long and distinguished career in animated films, Jones received an Academy Award for Lifetime Achievement in 1996. Yet as Jones freely admitted, when he left Chouinard back in 1930, all he wanted was to find a job that would enable him to eat three square meals a day.

An Introduction to Animation

In 1930 Jones headed for Paris, France, to pursue a career as a painter. But he arrived in France in the midst of the Great Depression, when countries all around the world were struggling with poverty and massive unemployment. In 1931 he returned to the United States, where he applied for a job at an animation studio. The studio hired him to work as a "cel-washer," wiping the drawings off of sheets of celluloid so that they could be used again in producing new cartoons. Jones's new job as a cel-washer was considered the lowliest one in the entire animation field. But by studying and simply being around these drawings, he was able learn much about this exciting art form. Later, he was promoted to the position of "in-be-tweener," a term used to describe the artist who draws hundreds of images based on poses created by other artists. When these hundreds of similar images are shot individually then linked together on film, they make the animated characters appear as if they are moving. In his free time, mean-while, Jones worked for an animation studio headed by Walter Lantz (who would later go on to create Woody Woodpecker) and as a portrait artist.

Jones once remarked that Pepé Le Pew was "everything I wanted to be romantically. Not only was he quite sure of himself, but it never occurred to him that anything was wrong with him. I always felt that there must be great areas of me that were repugnant to girls, and Pepé was quite the opposite of that."

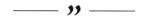

At the urging of his friend and future wife Dorothy, Jones took a job with the Leon Schlesinger Studio in 1933. This unit produced short animated films that Schlesinger licensed to the Warner Brothers film company so that they could be shown before their feature films. Jones soon began work-ing in a rundown building lovingly called Termite Terrace. He worked side by side with giants in the field of ani-mation, like Tex Avery, Bob Clampett, Frank Tashlin, Friz Freleng, and Robert McKimson, all of whom were working on the "Looney Tunes" and "Merrie Melodies" cartoon series. Jones soaked up all the knowledge that these men and others had to offer and eventual-ly got his first animation credit work-ing on a Freleng short cartoon enti-tled *The Miller's Daughter*. Later, Jones would develop a close working relationship with Avery, an animation di-rector known for his outlandish comedy. In regards to Avery, Jones once recalled that "He was only at Warners from 1933 to 1942, but he had an immense effect. He had an exquisite sense of what you might call 'ridicu-lous timing.' He's the only man I know who can do things that I wouldn't even begin to try."

Jones eventually earned the opportunity to make animated films of his own. These early films adopted a "cutesy" style that was similar to the works being produced by Walt Disney. As Steve Schneider wrote, "[Chuck Jones's] *Tom Thumb in Trouble* was the most Disney-like of all Warner car-

Pepé Le Pew, undated still

toons; virtually humorless, this sentimental tale even boasts an original song." Jones later claimed that this was a necessary period of growth for him. "It was a learning time for me," he explained. "I wasn't quite satisfied with the quality of the animation then. That's why so many of my early pictures are so slow—I was trying to find out how to do it."

In 1938, Jones finally got a chance to direct his first cartoon, *The Night Watchman*. One year later, Jones introduced one of his first original animated characters—a mouse named Sniffles—in *Naughty But Mice*. Sniffles was subsequently featured in many cartoons over the next seven years (the last being *Hush My Mouse* in 1946), but he never really became popular.

In *The Dover Boys* (1942), however, Jones used innovative character movements and backgrounds that greatly impressed other veterans of the cartoon industry. They recognized that these breakthroughs could only have been developed by an enormously talented and ambitious artist. For his part, Jones insisted that cartoon movement was an essential ingredient in animated filmmaking. "Movement is how animation acts," he said. "What makes a cartoon character significant is not how it looks, it's how it moves." This philosophy served as a springboard for Jones and his contemporaries, who were increasingly focusing their creative energy on the development of new animated personalities in the Looney Tunes stable.

A Fine Cast of Characters

By the late 1930s, some of the characters that had been developed at Schlesinger's studio were emerging as cartoon superstars. Among them were Tex Avery's Porky Pig, Bugs Bunny (created by Charles Thorson but fleshed out by Avery), Daffy Duck, and Elmer Fudd. While Jones didn't create these cartoon characters, he did have a tremendous influence on their development. It was with Daffy Duck that Jones would have some of his earliest successes. Originally the character was conceived as nothing more than a crazy screwball, but Jones infused him with a complex personality that included strong doses of greed, insecurity, and determination. In fact, Jones utilized Daffy almost as if he was an actor, casting him in a variety of roles including detective, swashbuckler, cowboy, astronaut, and even the legendary Robin Hood.

> *Jones insisted that cartoon movement was an essential ingredient in animated filmmaking. "Movement is how animation acts. What makes a cartoon character significant is not how it looks, it's how it moves."*

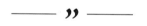

Jones and his fellow animators also gave Daffy Duck his voice, supplied by the legendary vocal artist Mel Blanc. Originally, Daffy Duck had said nothing but "Woo-Hoo" as he bounced around creating havoc. But Jones and the others decided that he should speak with a strong lisp like their boss Leon Schlesinger, whom they all disliked. Schlesinger never recognized that he was being insulted, however. Instead, he praised the reworked Daffy Duck as a hilarious character.

Jones also reworked the personality of Bugs Bunny. Jones decided to make him more of a heroic type: brash and sarcastic, yet cool and sophisticated. "He is also that unusual comedian: a comic hero, and they are very few," Jones revealed. "Bugs is what I would like to be: debonair, quick-witted, very fast on the comeback." Bugs often finds himself in plenty of trouble,

Characters that Jones Created	Characters that Jones Helped to Develop	
Crawford	Bugs Bunny	Elmer Fudd
Gossamer	Claude Cat	Porky Pig
Henery Hawk	Daffy Duck	
Hugo the Abdominable Snowman	**Characters that Jones Adapted from Print**	
Junyer Bear		
Marc Antony Kitty		
Marvin Martian	Chester Cricket	Mowgli
Pepé Le Pew	Dot and Line	Milo
Ralph Wolf	Grinch	Pogo
Road Runner	Harry Cat	Raggedy Ann
Sam Sheepdog	Horton the Elephant	Raggedy Andy
Sniffles	Kotick the White Seal	Rikki-Tikki-Tavi
Wile E. Coyote		

From Chuck Amuck *by Chuck Jones.*

but usually because he is provoked, and he always comes out on top. "In every film," explained Jones, "someone must have designs upon his person: [as food], as a trophy, as a good-luck piece (rabbit's foot, which makes as much sense as a rabbit carrying a human foot on a key chain), as an unwilling participant in scientific experiments. Without such threats, Bugs is far too capable a rabbit to evoke the necessary sympathy." Jones's version of Bugs Bunny served as the model for the other directors at Termite Terrace, but each director emphasized a different aspect of Bugs Bunny's personality. For example, in films directed by Jones, Bugs Bunny was clever and intellectual. By contrast, Friz Freleng's version of Bugs Bunny was a bit more zany and slapstick in tone. Still, all of the directors made sure that they kept Bugs's confident and appealing personality intact.

In 1944, Schlesinger decided to retire and sold his studio to Warner Bros. Schlesinger made a lot of money on this deal, but the men who had developed the studio's famous cartoon characters received little compensation for their years of hard work. "Each of the directors got a gold pen and a gold pencil for all their years of working for Leon. And he had us to dinner at his house for the first time," Jones later recalled.

"Hip Hip-Hurry!" 1958

Working for Warner Bros.

After joining Warner Bros., Jones created original characters that eventually rivaled the popularity of Bugs Bunny and Daffy Duck. Among them was Pepé Le Pew, a stinky French skunk who thinks he is a great lover but actually repulses all around him. Pepé was introduced in 1945 in *Odor-Able Kitty*, but became a star in 1947 in *Scent-imental Over You*, which earned Jones his first Academy Award. Ironically, Warner Bros. executive Eddie Selzer originally forbade Jones to work on the character because he didn't personally understand it. Thankfully, Jones had a habit of ignoring his bosses and doing his own thing.

In 1949, Jones and writer Michael Maltese created two of the most popular Warner Bros. cartoon characters ever: the Road Runner and Wile E. Coyote. Their debut film, entitled *Fast and Furry-ous*, initially started out as a parody of chase cartoons. In it, the Coyote constantly pursued the Road Runner across a bleak desert landscape, using a variety of gadgets supplied by a fictional company known as Acme. Despite his valiant efforts, however, the Road Runner always escaped and the Coyote usually ended up in some sort of physical pain. The cartoon featured no dialogue except for the Road Runner's occasional "Beep Beep."

The film was a complete success, but a follow-up wasn't produced immediately because the executives at Warner Bros. did not think the concept was funny. The pair was not seen again until *Beep Beep* in 1952, but by this time the public reaction was so great that the series went into regular production. In all, 26 cartoons were produced in the series and each one followed the same format and rules: the Coyote never caught the Road Runner, the Road Runner never left the road, and all of the pain that was inflicted on the Coyote was completely of his own doing.

In addition to Pepé Le Pew, Road Runner, and Wile E. Coyote, Jones personally created several other notable characters including Marvin Martian, Henery Hawk, Gossamer, Junyer Bear, Marc Antony Kitty, Pussyfoot, Sam Sheepdog, and Ralph Wolf (who, aside from his red nose, looked exactly like Wile E. Coyote).

Jones seemed to infuse a bit of his own personality into his characters. "I never had to leave home to develop any character I ever developed or helped to develop," he once said. "All I had to do was reach down inside my own self and there lurking was the essence of Daffy Duck, the Coyote, or Elmer, or the Martian. It was simply a matter of bringing it to the surface."

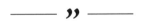

In all of Jones's work with Warner Bros., he seemed to infuse a bit of his own personality into his characters. "I never had to leave home to develop any character I ever developed or helped to develop," he once said. "All I had to do was reach down inside my own self and there lurking was the essence of Daffy Duck, the Coyote, or Elmer, or the Martian. It was simply a matter of bringing it to the surface." For example, Jones once remarked that Pepé Le Pew was "everything I wanted to be romantically. Not only was he quite sure of himself, but it never occurred to him that anything was wrong with him. I always felt that there must be great areas of me that were repugnant to girls, and Pepé was quite the opposite of that." In regards to Wile E. Coyote, Jones remarked "the Coyote is a history of my own frustration and war with all tools, multiplied only slightly." But when it came to his true inner self, Jones would later confess that "at night I dream of being Bugs Bunny, but when I wake up I'm Daffy Duck."

The Classic Films of Chuck Jones

The films of this era solidified Jones's place in animation history. In 1995, more than 1,000 animators, cartoon historians, and animation professionals were asked to rate their favorite cartoon films of all time for a book edited by Jerry Beck, entitled *The Fifty Greatest Cartoons*. Jones's name dominated the list, securing four of the top five spots. Jones's *What's Opera, Doc?* (1957), which condensed Richard Wagner's 14-hour opera *Ring of the Nibelungs* into a frantic six minutes, was ranked first on the list. A highly originally work, it features Bugs Bunny in the role of Brunhilde and Elmer Fudd as the Viking Siegfried. Bugs later dresses in drag as the Rhinemaiden and the pair dance a ballet and duet to an original song entitled "Return My Love." Jones also took the second spot in the poll with *Duck Amuck* (1953), which featured Daffy Duck at war with his animator (who turned out to be Bugs Bunny). Those two films would later be inducted into the National Film Registry for being "among the most culturally, historically, and aesthetically significant films of our time."

In regards to Wile E. Coyote, Jones remarked "the Coyote is a history of my own frustration and war with all tools, multiplied only slightly." But when it came to his true inner self, Jones would later confess that "at night I dream of being Bugs Bunny, but when I wake up I'm Daffy Duck."

Daffy appeared again in the film that rated number four, *Duck Dodgers in the 24 1/2 Century* (1953). This futuristic cartoon directed by Jones features Daffy and his sidekick Porky Pig doing battle with Marvin Martian over the discovery of Planet X, home to the extremely rare shaving cream atom. The number five film, Jones's *One Froggy Evening* (1956), was once hailed by film director Steven Spielberg as the cartoon equivalent of the classic film *Citizen Kane*, which is regarded by many critics as the best film ever made. *One Froggy Evening* has no dialogue and features a character called Michigan J. Frog, an amphibian with the ability to sing and dance. The problem is that he will only perform for his construction worker owner, who wishes to exploit the frog for his own financial gain. This situation causes the poor man eventually to go bankrupt and finally insane.

Jones also placed six more cartoons in this exclusive list, including *Rabbit of Seville* (1950) at number 12. This film, a parody of the classic Rossini opera

The Barber of Seville, featured Bugs Bunny tormenting Elmer Fudd in a variety of barber-related ways. *Rabbit Seasoning* (1952), which placed 30th, was the second of the classic "Rabbit Season! Duck Season!" trilogy in which Bugs Bunny and Daffy Duck scheme to get the befuddled hunter Elmer Fudd to blow the other to smithereens. *The Scarlet Pumpernickel* (1950) came in at number 31, and featured Daffy Duck as an actor trying to land a swashbuckling role. *Ali Baba Bunny* (1957), ranked 35, featured Bugs and Daffy interacting with a Genie. In *Feed the Kitty* (1952), a brutish bulldog named Marc Antony falls in love with a sweet black kitten and then tries to hide it from his owner. When the dog fears that the kitten has been killed, he breaks down weeping in a scene that is both touching and hilarious at the same time. This film placed 36th on the list. Finally, Jones's innovative 1942 film *The Dover Boys* (1942) came in at number 49.

Work Away from Warner Bros.

In 1955, Jack Warner — the head of the Warner Bros. studio — decided that all movies should be filmed in 3-D (three-dimensional imagery), so he decided to close the animation department of the studio. Jones then took a job at Walt Disney Studio, where he worked for four months on the film *Sleeping Beauty*. When Warner's 3-D experiment failed, Jones returned to his old unit. When Walt Disney asked Jones why he was leaving, he replied, "There's only one job around here worth having — and that's yours!" To which Disney replied, "You're absolutely right. Unfortunately, it's full."

In 1963 Warner Bros. decided to close its animation studio permanently. Jones quickly formed his own production company, called Chuck Jones Enterprises. He was immediately hired by another film studio, Metro Goldwyn-Mayer (MGM), to direct their successful Tom and Jerry cartoon series. The cat and mouse pair, originally created by Joseph Hanna and William Barbera, was immensely popular. Over the next few years, Jones made several humorous and entertaining Tom and Jerry films, including 1964's *War and Pieces* and *Much Ado About Mousing*. But Jones later admitted that "I didn't do [Tom and Jerry] very well. Mine were more like the Road Runner and Coyote in drag, I guess. But I tried hard, and I really cared about them, trying to make them right. But I was really over there because that was the only place available at the time that would allow me to do character animation."

In 1965, Jones received another Academy Award for his film *The Dot and the Line*, but his biggest success away from Warner Bros. would not come until 1967. This time, Jones teamed up with children's author Dr. Seuss (real name Theodor Geisel) to produce an animated television special for

©1969 METRO-GOLDWYN-MAYER Inc.

The Phantom Tollbooth, *1971*

his story *How the Grinch Stole Christmas.* The program was a huge success and has since become an annual holiday television staple for viewers of all ages. Four years later, Jones and Geisel collaborated on a film adaptation of the author's *Horton Hears a Who.*

Jones finally got his chance to work on a feature length film in 1971, when he developed *The Phantom Tollbooth,* from the book by Norton Juster. Jones served as a producer, co-director, and co-writer for this MGM film, which was a critical success but had a lackluster performance at the box office. *The Phantom Tollbooth* would later become known as a cult favorite. This same year, Jones directed a television special based on Walt Kelly's classic comic strip *Pogo,* entitled *The Pogo Family Birthday Special.*

Jones took a stab at a television series in 1972 when he produced a short-lived cartoon series for the National Film Board of Canada entitled *Curiosity Shop.* Despite its lack of success, the experience of working on the show allowed Jones to infuse Saturday morning cartoons with a program that he felt was lacking at the time in shows like *Scooby-Doo* and *Rocky and Bullwinkle.* "What they're doing on Saturday morning is what I call 'Illustrated Radio,'" he complained. "They build a full dialogue and use as few drawings as they can. They anchor the heads on one cell; the lips move and the eyes blink, maybe. Occasionally, the heads turn, but everyone moves the same."

Soon thereafter, Jones would have better luck with a string of television specials that included *The Cricket in Times Square* and *A Very Merry Cricket* (1973); *Yankee Doodle Cricket and The White Seal* (1974); *Rikki-Tikki-Tavi* (1975); and *Carnival of Animals* and *Mowgli's Brothers* (1976). Jones also contributed animation to the live action films *Stay Tuned* (1992) and *Mrs. Doubtfire* (1993) and appeared as himself in *Gremlins* (1984).

Enjoying Life as a Famous Cartoonist

In Jones's later years, he found countless things to keep him busy. In the late 1970s, he founded the industry for signed limited edition animation cels. Since the original production cels for Jones's work had long since been destroyed, Jones licensed the characters from Warner Bros. and lovingly re-created classic scenes and sold them to collectors worldwide through private galleries and through his daughter's company, Linda Jones Enterprises. Initially, "They went for $15 to $25 each," Linda Jones Clough remarked in 1997. "Now, to my surprise, they sell for $2,500." Jones also produced oil paintings featuring the Looney Tunes characters during this time. In addition, Jones regularly traveled to colleges and universities around the world, giving lectures about his career and his animation philosophy. In 1989 he published his autobiography, *Chuck Amuck: The Life and Times of an Animated Cartoonist*. Two years later, he released a book about his life in animation called *Chuck Reducks: Drawing From the Fun Side of Life*.

———— 66 ————

Jones has been an inspiration to John Lasseter, head of Pixar Animation Studios (which has produced such films as Toy Story, A Bug's Life, *and* Monsters, Inc. *Lasseter said that "He had the greatest comic timing in all of cinema history, an ability to know just how long to hold something, from Wile E. Coyote falling (off a cliff) to the look on Daffy's face."*

———— 99 ————

As the years went on, Jones showed no signs that age was dragging down his famed creativity or ambition. "I have about 50 projects that I'll either do or die trying," he said in 1996 at age 84. "I have no interest in dying. I have no experience with it. I have no belief in death. I don't feel like an old man.

I feel like a young man that has something the matter with him. I have no fears of the future. I only have fears of the past being repeated."

On March 25, 1996, Jones received an Academy Award for lifetime achievement. Presented by comedian Robin Williams, the award paid tribute to his creation of "classic cartoons and cartoon characters whose animated lives have brought joy to our real ones for more than half a century." Jones was moved and delighted by the award. "It's shockingly wonderful to receive such an honor from one's peers," he said. "I deeply appreciate receiving it, not only for myself, but for the five directors who were the original unit on the Warner Bros. lot. I'm the only one left and I will proudly accept the award for all of us. We did more than 1,500 cartoons during those 30 years and it was truly an all-for-one, one-for-all situation." In August 2001, Jones received another honor. He was one of the first three inductees (along with Walt Disney and cartoon inventor Winsor McCay) into the Animation Hall of Fame.

> *Genndy Tartakovsky, creator of the cartoons "Dexter's Laboratory" and "Samurai Jack," also held Jones in high regard. "He looked at life and did his own version. That's what a great director does, like Coppola or Scorsese. They have signatures. You can watch a cartoon, and halfway through you'll realize: This is a Chuck Jones picture."*

While Jones cherished these honors and the considerable success he had achieved away from Warner Bros., he still yearned to return to the characters that he knew and loved so well. Years before, the studio had destroyed all of his original cartoon art to make way for storage space. Jones had long since forgiven Warner Bros. for this desecration. He had even come to terms with the studio's decision to sell the TV rights to the characters and stories he helped create at a cheap rate. He just wanted to work with his old friends again.

In 1993 Jones got his wish when Chuck Jones Film Productions, the production company he formed with his daughter Linda, reached agreement with Warner Bros. to make a new batch of cartoons featuring the classic Looney Tunes characters. "My job, as I understand it, is to develop the same spirit that existed (then) and have new adventures with the old characters and new adventures with new characters," declared Jones. Over the

THE BUGS BUNNY / ROAD RUNNER MOVIE

The Bugs Bunny / Road Runner Movie, *1979*

next four years, Jones and his fellow animators produced *Chariots of Fur*, starring the Road Runner and Wile E. Coyote; *Superior Duck*, starring Daffy Duck; *Pullet Surprise*, starring Foghorn Leghorn and Pete Puma; and *Another Froggy Evening*, which marked the second appearance of the popular Michigan J. Frog. Unfortunately, the studio was closed by Warner Bros. in 1997. But the following year, Jones further cemented his relationship with Warner Bros. when he signed a lifetime contract with the studio to promote their animated characters. At the time, he proudly proclaimed, "They can't fire me 'til I'm dead."

Recently Jones was working on a new cartoon series featuring an original character for the Warner Bros. website. The new cartoons debuted in April 2002, shortly after the death of their creator. The web films, which Jones originally had hoped to get into theaters, feature a luckless wolf named Thomas T. (for "Timber") Wolf who is smashed by a tree every time someone mentions his middle name.

The Passing of a Legend

On February 22, 2002, Jones died of congestive heart failure at the age of 89 at his home in Corona Del Mar, California. As word of his passing moved through Hollywood, those who were influenced by him were quick to pay tribute. "Chuck's originality, humor, and pacing have no peer," film director Steven Spielberg said. Rob Minkoff, one of the directors of Disney's *The Lion King*, remarked: "He always looked for something a bit edgier. There's a vitality, an aliveness to his work." His work has been an inspiration to John Lasseter, head of Pixar Animation Studios (which has produced such films as *Toy Story*, *A Bug's Life*, and *Monsters, Inc.*). Lasseter said that "He had the greatest comic timing in all of cinema history, an ability to know just how long to hold something, from Wile E. Coyote falling (off a cliff) to the look on Daffy's face." Genndy Tartakovsky, creator of "Dexter's Laboratory" and "Samurai Jack," also held Jones in high regard. "He looked at life and did his own version. That's what a great director does, like Coppola or Scorsese. They have signatures. You can watch a cartoon, and halfway through you'll realize: This is a Chuck Jones picture."

MARRIAGE AND FAMILY

Jones married Dorothy Webster on January 31, 1935, and they were together for 43 years until her death in 1978. The couple had one daughter, Linda Jones Clough, who had three children of her own: Todd, Craig, and Valerie. Jones's three grandchildren would later give him six great-grandchildren. On January 14, 1983, Jones married writer Marian Dern, who had two children, Peter and Rosalin, from a previous marriage. Soon thereafter, Marian Dern reassumed her maiden name, which just happened to be Jones.

SELECTED WORKS

Books

Rikki-Tikki-Tavi, 1982 (Illustrator)
The White Seal, 1982 (Illustrator)
The Cricket in Times Square, 1984 (Illustrator)
Mowgli's Brothers, 1985 (Illustrator).
William the Backwards Skunk, 1987 (Author and Illustrator)
Chuck Amuck: The Life and Times of an Animated Cartoonist, 1989 (Author)
Chuck Reducks: Drawing From the Fun Side of Life, 1991 (Author)
"What's Up, Down Under?" Essay in *The Illusion of Life: Essays on Animation,* 1991
Chuck Jones' Peter and the Wolf, 1994 (Illustrator)
Daffy Duck for President, 1997 (Author and Illustrator)

Feature Films and Television Specials (as director and producer)

Gay Purr-ee, 1962
How the Grinch Stole Christmas, 1970
The Phantom Tollbooth, 1971
Horton Hears a Who, 1971
The Pogo Special Birthday Special, 1971

A Christmas Carol, 1973 (executive producer)
The Cricket in Times Square, 1973
A Very Merry Cricket, 1973
Yankee Doodle Cricket, 1974
The White Seal, 1974
Rikki-Tikki-Tavi, 1975
Carnival of the Animals, 1976
Mowgli's Brothers, 1976
Bugs Bunny in King Arthur's Court, 1978
Raggedy Ann and Andy in the Great Santa Claus Caper, 1978
The Bugs Bunny/Roadrunner Movie, 1979
Daffy Duck's Thanks for Giving Special, 1979
Bugs Bunny's Looney Christmas Tales, 1979
The Pumpkin Who Couldn't Smile, 1979
Bugs Bunny's Bustin' Out All Over, 1980
Duck Dodgers and the Return of the 24½ Century, 1980

Chuck Jones also directed more than 230 short animated films for Warner Bros. (WB) and Metro-Goldwyn-Mayer (MGM) over the course of his career.

HONORS AND AWARDS

Academy Awards

Director, Best Animated Cartoon: 1950, for *For Scent-imental Reasons*
Director, Best Documentary Short Subject: 1950, for *So Much for So Little*
Director, Best Animated Cartoon: 1965, for *The Dot and the Line*
Academy Award for Lifetime Achievement: 1996

Other Major Awards

Great Director Award (U.S.A. Film Festival): 1986
Best Animation Award (National Society of Cartoonists): 1986, 1987, 1988, 1990
Lifetime Achievement Award (Chicago Film Festival): 1987
Lifetime Achievement Award (Houston Film Festival): 1988
Lifetime Achievement Award (Zagreb Film Festival): 1988
Golden Plate Award (American Academy of Achievement): 1990
Career Achievement Award (Los Angeles Critics): 1991
Lifetime Achievement Award (Denver Film Festival): 1996
Honorary Life Membership Award (Directors Guild of America): 1996
Smithsonian Institution 150th Anniversary Medal of Achievement: 1996

Inducted into International Museum of Cartoon Art Hall of Fame: 1997
Edward MacDowell Medal: 1997
Inducted into Art Directors Club Hall of Fame: 1998
Chevalier des Arts et Lettres Award (France Ministry of Culture): 1998
Lifetime Achievement Award (Santa Clarita Film Festival): 1999
Inducted into Animation Hall of Fame: 2001

FURTHER READING

Books

American Animated Cartoon, 1980
Authors and Artists for Young Adults, Vol. 2, 1989
Bogdanovich, Peter. *Who the Devil Made It,* 1997
Broughton, Irv. *Producers on Producing: The Making of Film and Television,* 1986
Cholodenko, Alan. *The Illusion of Life: Essays on Animation,* 1991
Contemporary Authors, New Revision Series, Vol. 106, 2002
Grant, John. *Masters of Animation,* 2001
Jones, Chuck. *Chuck Amuck: The Life and Times of an Animated Cartoonist,* 1989
Jones, Chuck. *Chuck Reducks: Drawing From the Fun Side of Life,* 1991
Peary, Danny, and Gerald Peary. *The American Animated Cartoon: A Critical Anthology,* 1980
Schneider, Steve. *That's All Folks! The Art of Warner Bros. Animation,* 1988
Something About the Author, Vol. 53, 1988

Periodicals

Animation Magazine, Jan. 2001, p.31
Atlantic, Dec. 1984, p.124
Current Biography Yearbook, 1996
Daily News of Los Angeles, Sep. 24, 1997
Entertainment Weekly, Mar. 8, 2002, p.22
Film Comment, Jan.-Feb. 1975, p.21
Los Angeles Times, Apr. 10, 1995, p.F2; Feb. 25, 2001, p.F11
New York Times, Oct. 7, 1979, p.D17; Aug. 9, 1992; Nov. 19, 2000, p.37; Feb. 24, 2002, p.L34
People, Nov. 13, 1989, p.103; Mar. 11, 2002, p.88
Publishers Weekly, Aug. 12, 1996, p.71
San Francisco Chronicle, Dec. 24, 1989, Datebook sec., p.30
Sight and Sound, Apr. 2002, p.3
South Florida Sun Sentinel, Mar. 3, 2002, p.1D

Star Tribune (Minneapolis, MN), June. 3, 1999, p.E1
Time, May 12, 1997, p.78; Mar. 4, 2002, p.80
Times (London), Feb. 25, 2002, p.39
Variety, Mar. 4, 2002, p.62
Washington Post, Feb. 25, 1980, p.B1

Online Articles

http://www.cartoon.org/jones.htm
   (*International Museum of Cartoon Art,* "Chuck Jones," undated)

Online Database

Biography Resource Center, 2002, article reproduced from *Contemporary Authors,* 2002

WORLD WIDE WEB SITE

http://www.chuckjones.com

Robert Lipsyte 1938-
American Sportswriter and Author for Young Adults
Author of *The Contender*
Winner of the 2001 Margaret A. Edwards Award for
Lifetime Achievement

BIRTH

Robert Michael Lipsyte was born on January 16, 1938, in New York City. His parents were Sidney and Fanny Lipsyte, both of whom worked in the field of education. Sidney Lipsyte was a school principal who later served as director of the New York City Bureau for the Education of Emotionally Disturbed and

Maladjusted Children. Lipsyte's mother was a teacher and guidance counselor. Lipsyte has one younger sister.

YOUTH

Lipsyte grew up in a middle-class Jewish neighborhood in Queens, a section of New York City. As a child, he participated in a wide variety of activities, from playing the piano and accordion to outdoor-oriented events with the Cub Scouts. But Lipsyte grew up in a home environment geared toward reading and learning, and these were the things that he found he enjoyed doing the most.

> ────── " ──────
>
> *As a young teenager, Lipsyte recalls, "[I] hated my body and hated to go out in the world. I was the marginalized boy. . . . You know, if you were fat or disabled or had very thick glasses or a stutter or whatever it was, that put you last to be chosen on the team and sent to play with the girls. So books and writing were a real refuge for me."*
>
> ────── " ──────

"I didn't go to ball games with my father," he recalled. "I went to the library with my father. That was our thing. We went to cowboy movies and we went to the library at least once a week. And I could take out as many books as I could carry. . . . So reading was very much encouraged in the household." Years later, he even admitted that he did not follow professional baseball, football, or basketball with the same interest that his peers showed. "I was never an avid spectator sports fan," he said. "Although I grew up in New York while there were still three major league baseball teams in town, I didn't attend my first game until I was 13 years old. I was profoundly disappointed. . . . I went to only one more game as a paying customer. The third one I covered for the *New York Times*."

As Lipsyte grew older, he became very overweight. The extra pounds made him a target for cruel treatment from classmates and peers and excluded him from many athletic activities. Not surprisingly, Lipsyte became very self-conscious about his appearance, and he avoided contact with other youngsters his own age. "[I] hated my body and hated to go out in the world," he acknowledged. "I was the marginalized boy. I was a girl. You know, if you were fat or disabled or had very thick glasses or a stutter or whatever it was, that put you last to be chosen on the team and sent to play with the girls. So books and writing were a real refuge for me."

During his early teen years, Lipsyte continued to spend much of his time by himself, reading books and writing his own short stories. He began to feel more at home in the fictional worlds of authors like John Steinbeck, Richard Halliburton, and J.D. Salinger, as well as in the worlds he himself was creating. These early writing efforts marked his first steps towards a career as an author and journalist. "Writing fiction has always been the most enjoyable thing I ever wanted to do," he later said. "It was the only thing I ever wanted to do, certainly since I was 11 or 12."

Lipsyte finally lost some of his extra weight at the age of 14, when he accepted a regular summer job doing yardwork for a local man. In fact, he lost more than 30 pounds over the course of a few months. "That summer, I left most of the worst of me on the lawn of a curmudgeon [cranky old man] who paid me a dollar an hour to mow, trim, rake, and clean the land around his country house. He delighted in humiliating me, especially in front of his guests, for blades of grass I failed to cut. I hated him then and I love him now. When I returned to school that September, my clothes hung on me like dead sails. I remember standing on the scale for what seemed like hours, smiling down at 168."

Lipsyte admits that his life became much more enjoyable in the years following his physical transformation. He was able to participate in sports that he had previously avoided, and classmates no longer badgered him about his appearance. "When I lost my weight at the age of 14, it was like those operations where a kid's blind all his life and then suddenly, 'I can see!'" he recalled. "And from the age of 14 for the next I don't know how many years, I didn't read, I didn't do anything, except, you know, play ball and screw around."

EDUCATION

Lipsyte was an exceptional student who participated in a program called the "Special Progress Class" for advanced students. He also channeled his writing talents into his elementary school literary magazine and the student newspaper at Forest Hills High School in Queens.

Lipsyte's participation in the accelerated learning program enabled him to skip his senior year of high school and enroll at the prestigious Columbia University in New York City. Upon graduating from Columbia in 1957, he initially planned to attend graduate school at Pomona-Claremont College in California to pursue a degree in romantic English poetry. But he decided to stay in New York when he secured a job in the sports department at the *New York Times*. Lipsyte later earned a master's degree in journalism from Columbia while working at the *Times*.

CAREER HIGHLIGHTS

Robert Lipsyte has made his mark in the literary world in a number of ways. In the 1960s he became a nationally syndicated sports columnist with a reputation for honestly examining unattractive aspects of America's fascination with sports. He also made critically acclaimed contributions to several television and radio programs over the years. In addition, he is the author of several highly regarded novels for young adults, including *The Contender.* Finally, he established himself as a respected authority on sports-related literature for young people. But Lipsyte managed all of these professional accomplishments only because he was willing to pay his dues as a writer for the *New York Times,* one of America's best newspapers.

"

"Writing under a deadline is often exhilarating," Lipsyte says about his years as a journalist. *"And if you're lucky and the event has moved you, a rhythm develops and the story just flows out of the typewriter."*

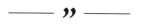

"

Becoming a Sports Reporter for the *New York Times*

Lipsyte's first job at the paper was as a copy boy. His work consisted of sharpening pencils, fetching food, and running errands for the sportswriters in the department. Despite his lowly position in the sports department *Times,* Lipsyte quickly fell in love with the hustle and bustle of the newsroom and the overall "romance of newspapering." In time, he began compiling statistics for the reporters, covering high school sports on his own, and writing short feature stories. The newspaper's editors took note of Lipsyte's enthusiasm and writing talent. In 1959 they promoted him to the position of full-time sports reporter, an amazing achievement for a 21-year-old.

Lipsyte worked as an apprentice reporter for three years before the newspaper started giving him regular assignments in 1962. His first major assignment was to go to Florida and cover spring training for the New York Mets, who were just beginning their inaugural season as a major league baseball team. Lipsyte was eager and enthusiastic about this opportunity. "I wanted to get out there and see what was going on and write better stories about it than anyone else," he remembered. This initial assignment taught him many things about being a journalist, including how to deal with deadlines and space constraints. "Writing under a deadline is often exhilarating," he would later remark. "And if you're lucky and the event has moved you, a rhythm develops and the story just flows out of the typewriter."

In 1964 Lipsyte took his first step into the professional world of books when he worked with Dick Gregory, an African-American comedian and political activist. He helped Gregory write his autobiography, entitled *Nigger*. During this same period, he emerged as one of the leading authorities at the *New York Times* on the sport of boxing. He developed friendships with heavyweight boxer Cassius Clay (later known as Muhammad Ali) and the famed boxing trainer Cus D'Amato during this period, and in the mid-1960s he wrote about the colorful Clay more than any other single athlete.

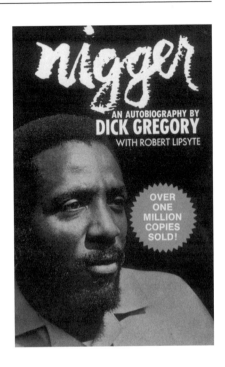

Becoming a *Contender*

At the time Lipsyte first met D'Amato, the trainer was more than twice his age. D'Amato had plenty of stories to tell from his years in the boxing world, and the young reporter soaked them up. One particular story had a strong effect on Lipsyte. D'Amato told him that he could tell if a young fighter had the potential to be a contender just by listening to the sound of his footsteps as he entered the ghetto gym that D'Amato owned. "At night, he would sit by the door, listening to prospective boxers come up three dark, narrow, twisting flights of stairs," recalled Lipsyte. "If he heard only one set of footsteps (the kid was alone) and if the footsteps were hesitant (he was conquering fear), there was a chance the kid might stay with it, hang tough, find himself through the act of dedication to a goal."

D'Amato's stories and knowledge inspired Lipsyte to write a young adult (YA) novel about a desperate young boxer. The final result was *The Contender*, a gritty story about a young African-American man named Alfred Brooks who feels that his only ticket out of the ghetto is to become a boxing champion. In the end, Brooks fails at his ultimate goal. But along the way, he learns some hard lessons about being a man and about the importance of doing something productive with his life.

Upon its publication in 1967, *The Contender* was an immediate commercial and critical success. It was hailed for its realistic depictions of the boxing culture and the issues of poverty, violence, drugs, and hopelessness that

were destroying many urban neighborhoods at that time. *Book World,* for instance, praised it as "a fine book in which interest combines with compassion and enlightenment." Lipsyte biographer Michael Cart, meanwhile, called *The Contender* a "compellingly readable sports story" that "is a tribute to the power of friendship and a celebration of brotherhood. It is also a testimonial to Lipsyte's own compassionate heart and social conscience."

In the meantime, the *New York Times* rewarded Lipsyte for his years of quality work with the opportunity to write a regular sports column for the paper. He was delighted with the offer. From 1967 to 1971 he wrote three commentaries a week on all sorts of sports-related subjects, from the fortunes of New York's professional sports teams to the increased influence of wealth and celebrity on the American sports scene.

Covering the World of Sports — Good and Bad

In 1970 Lipsyte collected some of his favorite newspaper columns and stories into a single volume titled *Assignment: Sports.* By presenting his writing in this way, he was able to show how his work differed from that of most other sportswriters. The collection — which featured fascinating personalities, sharp dialogue, interesting settings, and strong opinions about politics, race relations, and power — received strong reviews. "[Lipsyte has] the skill of a fine fiction writer," observed the *New York Times Book Review.* "Readers meeting him for the first time, regardless of age group, have a rare treat in store."

The following year, Lipsyte decided that it was time for him to step away from the world of sports journalism. He resigned from the *New York Times* in the fall of 1971 and devoted his writing energies toward a series of book projects. "I knew I'd miss the quick excitement of deadline journalism," he admitted. "But I wanted more time to think about what I had seen during the past 14 years, and more space to shape those thoughts into characters and stories."

In the early 1970s Lipsyte published two novels for adult audiences — *Something Going* in 1972 (co-written with Steve Cady) and *Liberty Two* in 1974. Neither of these works attracted much attention from critics or readers. But in 1975 he published a nonfiction book — *SportsWorld: An American Dreamland* — that stirred up a blizzard of critical acclaim and controversy.

In *SportsWorld,* Lipsyte drew upon his years of experience as a sportswriter to condemn the dominant American attitudes towards sports, competition, and athletes. The book used the term "SportsWorld" to represent the current state of sports in American culture. In Lipsyte's opinion, the world of sports had degenerated from its original, pure form and become characterized by greed and an excessive thirst for power and fame. "Sometime in the last 50 years the sports experience was perverted into a SportsWorld state of mind in which the winner was good because he won; the loser, if not actually bad, was at least reduced, and had to prove himself over again, through competition," he declared. "SportsWorld is a grotesque distortion of sports. . . . It has made the finish more important than the race. . . . By the end of the 1960s, SportsWorld wisdom had it that religion was a spectator sport while professional and college athletic contests were the only events Americans held sacred."

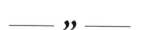

"Sometime in the last 50 years the sports experience was perverted into a SportsWorld state of mind in which the winner was good because he won; the loser, if not actually bad, was at least reduced, and had to prove himself over again, through competition. SportsWorld is a grotesque distortion of sports. . . . By the end of the 1960s, SportsWorld wisdom had it that religion was a spectator sport while professional and college athletic contests were the only events Americans held sacred."

Reaction to *SportsWorld* was swift and strong. Some critics accused Lipsyte of hating sports or ignoring positive aspects of modern sports. "I admired his column and I wanted to like his book," commented one reviewer in the *New York Times Book Review*. "But *SportsWorld* lacks a sense of joy [about athletic competition]." Many other reviewers rushed to Lipsyte's defense, however. *Newsweek,* for example, called it a "persuasive volume" that "sparkles with insightful portraits of figures ranging from the self-protectively spaced-out Kareem Abdul-Jabbar to Muhammad Ali, Lipsyte's premiere subject throughout his journalistic career. . . . For all his disaffection, Lipsyte still loves sports. He only laments our transformation into a nation of sideline fantasists. . . . Read him, and you will never look at a sports event in quite the same way again." Lipsyte biographer Michael Cart, meanwhile, insisted that "*SportsWorld* is beautifully, even artfully written. . . . It is filled with observed moments of humor and with witty writing. . . . Whether readers agree or disagree with Lipsyte's opinions in *SportsWorld* is moot [unimportant]. After all, the book's most enduring contribution to the literature of sports is that it invites, challenges, and stimulates the reader to think about the issues he raises."

Lipsyte Returns to YA Literature

In 1977, nearly ten years after publishing the young adult novel *The Contender*, Lipsyte published a second novel for young adults called *One Fat Summer*. The new book featured an overweight 14-year-old named Bobby Marks growing up in the 1950s. Drawing heavily upon his own adolescent experiences, Lipsyte created a central character that embodied the fears, feelings of inadequacy, and courage of countless teenage boys and girls all across the country. "I always thought that I would write about the summer I had lost a lot of weight and had never been able to," Lipsyte recalled. But by the mid-1970s, he was finally able to write about his experiences in

a positive way. "I really wanted to write about kids and their bodies," he explained. "While the pressures and feelings might have been different in the 1950s, the internal thoughts on how one viewed his or her own body and how one viewed oneself in relation to friends and parents probably never changed."

One Fat Summer was another big success for Lipsyte and further cemented his reputation as an author of quality literature for young adult audiences. Over the next few years, Lipsyte eventually produced two sequels to *One Fat Summer* that followed the maturation of Bobby Marks. In *Summer Rules* (1981), 16-year-old Marks is working as a camp counselor. But his summer erupts in emotional turmoil when he falls in love with a girl with an emotionally troubled younger brother. In *The Summerboy* (1982), 18-year-old Marks becomes embroiled in a fight for worker's rights while employed at a laundry.

Critics praised all three volumes of the Bobby Marks trilogy for their compelling storylines, convincing depictions of the 1950s, and realistic and compassionate treatment of teen issues. *Top of the News*, for example, commented that "Lipsyte's absorbing plots, strong characterizations, and insights into individuals' motivations create fine works of social realism." The

———— " ————

"I really liked him a lot,"
Lipyste said about his
character Bobby Marks from
One Fat Summer. *"I guess*
one of the reasons that I like
him is he was an idealized
extension of me; he was like
me, but better than me.
He was humorous and self-
deprecating. He was brave.
He was smart. He didn't al-
ways get what he wanted, but
he kept going. . . . I didn't
start out intending a trilogy,
but when I finished One Fat
Summer *I didn't feel a lot*
of relief. I was depressed, like
I'd moved out of the neigh-
borhood and left one of my
friends behind."

———— " ————

New York Times Book Review added that "refreshingly, [Bobby Marks] is neither precocious nor off-beat . . . but simply a normal boy in abnormal circumstances."

For his part, Lipsyte acknowledged that he was very fond of the Bobby Marks character. "I really liked him a lot," he said. "I guess one of the reasons that I like him is he was an idealized extension of me; he was like me, but better than me. He was humorous and self-deprecating [able to poke fun at himself]. He was brave. He was smart. He didn't always get what he wanted, but he kept going. . . . I didn't start out intending a trilogy, but when I finished *One Fat Summer* I didn't feel a lot of relief. I was depressed, like I'd moved out of the neighborhood and left one of my friends behind."

Diagnosed with Cancer

During the late 1970s Lipsyte maintained a busy professional schedule. In addition to continuing to write books, he worked for the *New York Post* and National Public Radio. In 1978, however, his professional and personal life were shaken by the news that he had been diagnosed with testicular cancer. Lipsyte soon had surgery followed by chemotherapy, a form of treatment that involves taking extremely strong medications that make people feel very sick. "Like most people, we regarded cancer as one of the most dread words in the language," he remembered. "If not a death sentence, we thought, at least it meant the end of a normal, productive life. We knew very little about cancer, but we learned quickly. After surgery, I underwent two years of chemotherapy. I was sick for a day or two after each treatment, and I lost some strength and some hair, but we were amazed at how normally my life continued: I wrote, I traveled, I swam and ran and played tennis. . . . When I finally stopped going for treatments, there was a hole in my routine. I felt in some ways like I lost a hobby."

Lipsyte was grateful that he could continue to play with his children, cover sports events, and write during his chemotherapy. But he admits that the violent nausea and sickness that comes with the treatment was difficult to endure. "When people say, 'You beat cancer,' I cringe. I believe that the nasty little cells are always inside you, waiting to ambush you until your immune system lets down. What I beat was chemo, two years of it. People sometimes quit chemo because it's a nasty business, you feel sicker than you did when the cancer was diagnosed."

Continuing His Work

In 1978 — the same year that he was first diagnosed with cancer — Lipsyte published a biography of boxer Muhammad Ali that was explicitly aimed at young adult audiences. *Free to Be Muhammad Ali* drew extensively from Lipsyte's experiences covering the fighter for the *New York Times* over the previous 14 years. For this book, Lipsyte detailed the life and career highlights of the heavyweight boxer, but he also tried to give readers a sense of Ali's beliefs and attitudes.

Lipsyte greatly enjoyed writing about Ali, who he described as "far and away the most interesting character in that mythical kingdom I call SportsWorld." Readers and critics, meanwhile, enjoyed reading *Free To Be Muhammad Ali*. The *New York Times Book Review*, for example, called it a "thoughtful, complex portrait of one of America's greatest athletes" and noted that the book reflects "the affection and respect the author feels for him as an athlete and a man."

Lipsyte's next young adult novel, published in 1982, was entitled *Jock and Jill*. This coming-of-age story features a high school pitcher named Jack Ryder who has a multitude of problems to

contend with as his team tries to win their local baseball championship. Poverty, drug abuse, and family turmoil are just a few of the challenges that Jack grapples with off of the baseball diamond.

Later in 1982, Lipsyte was approached by the television network CBS to contribute segments on sports and other subjects to their popular program "Sunday Morning." He accepted the offer and stayed with the program for the next four years. Lipsyte enjoyed this new challenge. "It would mean hitting the road again and writing on a deadline, learning a new field and meeting new people," he said. "It would be like starting over again." In 1986 he left CBS to join NBC News, but one year later he moved on to serve as host of a program called "The 11th Hour" on the public TV network PBS. The show was a huge critical success and won five Emmy awards. Unfortunately, "The 11th Hour" was canceled after only one year because of a cost cutting move at the publicly funded network.

Lipsyte enjoyed working on television and radio. But writing always remained his first and greatest professional love. "Television is fun—a friend of mine calls it a perpetual seventh-grade class trip—but nothing is as much fun as creating a world on a piece of paper, especially for readers whose minds are still open to change and possibility," he remarked.

Concentrating on Stories for Young Adults

In 1991 Lipsyte published a sequel to his 1967 YA novel *The Contender*. In this book, called *The Brave,* the young boxer Alfred Brooks is now a 40-year-old police officer fighting a drug war on the streets of New York. Brooks eventually meets Sonny Bear, a troubled young man who has run away from the Indian Reservation where he grew up. As the story proceeds, Brooks teaches the young man how to box, and in the process teaches him many lessons about life.

The third book in the series, *The Chief*, was published in 1993. This time, Sonny Bear's skills as a boxer have made him a highly regarded contender, but incidents of racial discrimination threaten to derail his career. He continues to be guided by Alfred Brooks, who has been crippled after suffering a bullet wound in the spine. *The Chief* is told from the viewpoint of Martin Witherspoon, a young African-American man who helps train Sonny and dreams of being a famous author. A fourth novel in the series, *The Warrior Angels*, is slated for publication in 2003.

In 1991, Lipsyte was diagnosed with a second case of testicular cancer and had to undergo chemotherapy once again. This time, Lipsyte decided that he would chronicle the ordeal in writing. For the next few years, he wrote regular columns in the *New York Times* and the magazine *American Health* describing his chemotherapy experiences and his feelings about fighting cancer. At the same time, he decided to write an entire book on the subject. "This time I would do what I hadn't done the first time—I would write about it. I would be the first man to write an honest book about cancer the second time around, a cancer whose treatment would cause me to reevaluate the meaning of manhood," he said. This work—*In the Country of Illness: Comfort and Advice for the Journey*—was published in 1998. It deals not only with his own experiences with the disease, but also with those of his second wife, Marjorie, who eventually died of cancer.

Even as he worked on *In the Country of Illness*, though, Lipsyte also continued to devote time to books for young adults. In 1992 he published *The Chemo Kid*, a fanciful story about a teenage cancer patient who develops superhuman powers as a result of the hormone treatments he receives during chemotherapy. He also wrote a series of sports biographies for younger readers, including *Arnold Schwarzenegger: Hercules in America* (1993), *Jim Thorpe: Twentieth-Century Jock* (1993), *Michael Jordan: A Life Above the Rim* (1994), and *Joe Louis: A Champ for All America* (1994). In 1995, Lipsyte joined with histo-

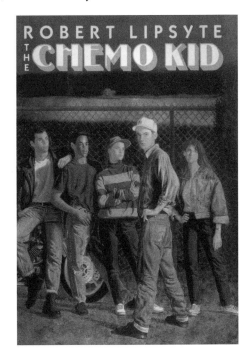

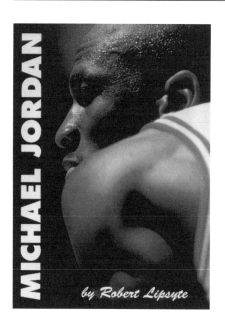

rian Peter Levine to write *Idols of the Game: A Sporting History of the American Century*. This work was produced not only as a book, but also as a six-hour television documentary series for the cable TV network TBS.

Children and Sports

Throughout the 1990s, Lipsyte also continued to speak out on a wide range of issues — from America's love affair with sports to the state of YA literature. For example, he remains highly critical of the nation's fascination with sports stars. He believes that famous athletes are often poor role models for young people, and that coverage of their exploits offers false hopes of stardom and riches to millions of children. Lipsyte also is convinced that American culture needs to recognize that athletic competition is just one aspect of a healthy life. "Sports is, or should be, just one of the things people do — an integral part of life, but only one aspect of it," he said. "Sports is a good experience. It's fun. It ought to be inexpensive and accessible to everybody."

Lipsyte contends that books for children and young adults can help teens understand that a good education and basic respect for others are far more important than the ability to run fast or throw a football accurately. "I don't think we have to make any rules for sports books for children beyond asking that they present some sense of truth about the role of sports in our lives," he said. "If we write more truthfully about sports, perhaps we can encourage kids to relax and have fun with each other — to challenge themselves for the pleasure of it, without self-doubt and without fear."

Lipsyte also believes that YA literature can be effective in helping young people explore their feelings about growing up in an uncertain and sometimes unfriendly world. "If kids are watching TV, if they're watching news programs, if they're watching soap operas, if they're watching prime time shows, then there is nothing in YA literature that can surprise or upset them," Lipsyte declared. "The point is that if YA literature is to have any moral value beyond enjoyment or entertainment, it's that it's telling kids that yes, these problems do exist in the world, and that people just like you, these characters in the books, are meeting them head on, are dealing with them. Sometimes they are succeeding completely, and sometimes they are being beaten down; just like life. . . . It's uplifting to know that there are other people who are facing the type of problems that you have to face. That's all you have to know. And then if the book can show you how some of these people overcome these problems, that's all the better."

Over the years, Lipsyte has received many awards for his work in print and on radio and television. But in 2001 he received his greatest honor yet, when he was awarded the American Library Association's coveted Margaret A. Edwards Award for Lifetime Achievement. The honor, bestowed in recognition of his long and distinguished participation in the world of young adult literature, pleased Lipsyte immensely. "The Edwards Award was kind of a championship," he said. "Winning a championship is a lot of luck—holding on to it is about hard work and talent. We'll see how good I am. I'm interested in finding out, too."

"I don't think we have to make any rules for sports books for children beyond asking that they present some sense of truth about the role of sports in our lives. If we write more truthfully about sports, perhaps we can encourage kids to relax and have fun with each other— to challenge themselves for the pleasure of it, without self-doubt and without fear."

MARRIAGE AND FAMILY

Lipsyte has been married three times. His first marriage ended in divorce in 1963. He remained close to his second wife, Marjorie Rubin, even after their divorce in 1987. Her losing battle with breast cancer was one of the events that inspired Lipsyte to write his book *In the Country of Illness.* Lipsyte married Katherine Lorraine Sulkes, a freelance television and news documentary producer, on August 22, 1992. Lipsyte has two children from his first marriage, a son named Sam and a daughter named Susannah. Sam Lipsyte later went on to become an author himself; he has published a short story collection and a novel.

WORKS

Fiction for Young Adults

The Contender, 1967
One Fat Summer, 1977

Summer Rules, 1981
Jock and Jill, 1982
The Summerboy, 1982
The Brave, 1991
The Chemo Kid, 1992
The Chief, 1993

Other Writings for Young Adults

Jim Thorpe: Twentieth-Century Jock, 1993
Arnold Schwarzenegger: Hercules in America, 1993
Michael Jordan: A Life Above the Rim, 1994
Joe Louis: A Champ for All America, 1994

Novels for Adults

Something Going, 1973 (with Steve Cady)
Liberty Two, 1974

Other Writings

Nigger, 1964 (with Dick Gregory)
The Masculine Mystique, 1966
Assignment: Sports, 1970; revised edition, 1984
SportsWorld: An American Dreamland, 1975
Free to Be Muhammad Ali, 1978
That's the Way of the World, 1975 (screenplay; also released under the title *Shining Star*)
Idols of the Game: A Sporting History of the American Century, 1995 (with Peter Levine)
In the Country of Illness: Comfort and Advice for the Journey, 1998

HONORS AND AWARDS

Dutton Best Sports Story Award: 1964, 1965, 1967, 1971, 1976
Mike Berger Award for Distinguished Reporting (Columbia University): 1966, 1996
Wel-Met Children's Book Award: 1967, for *The Contender*
Outstanding Children's Book of the Year (*New York Times*): 1977, for *One Fat Summer*
Best Young Adult Book (American Library Association): 1977, for *One Fat Summer*
Emmy Award for On-Camera Achievement: 1990, for *The 11th Hour*

Sports Journalist of the Year (*Village Voice* Sportswriter's Poll): 1991, 1999
ALAN Award for Contributions to Young Adult Literature: 1999
Margaret A. Edwards Award for Lifetime Achievement (American Library
  Association): 2001

FURTHER READING

Books

Authors and Artists for Young Adults, Vol. 7, 1991
Cart, Michael. *Presenting Robert Lipsyte,* 1995
Gallo, Donald R. *Speaking for Ourselves: Autobiographical Sketches by
  Notable Authors of Books for Young Adults,* 1990
Silvey, Anita. *Children's Books and Their Creators,* 1995
St. James Guide to Young Adult Writers, 1999
Twentieth-Century Young Adult Writers, 1994
Writers for Young Adults, 1997

Periodicals

American Health, July-Aug. 1991, p.32; Sep. 1991, p.26; Dec. 1991, p.31;
  Dec. 1992, p. 23; Apr. 1991, p.27; Mar. 1992, p.28
Book Links, Nov. 1992, p.38
Book World, Nov. 5, 1967, p.43
Booklist, Sep. 15, 1970, p.97
Bulletin of the Center for Children's Books, May 1968, p.145
Chicago Tribune, May 7, 1998, section: Tempo, p.3
Children's Literature in Education, Spring 1980, p.43
Elementary English, Jan. 1972, p.116
English Journal, Mar. 1987, p.16
Harper's Magazine, Sep. 1985, p.45
Horn Book, May-June, 1992, p.292
New York, Jan. 30, 1989, p.58
New York Times, June 15, 1986, p.29
New York Times Magazine, Jan. 13, 2002, section 8, p.11
New York Times Book Review, May 31, 1970, p.14; Nov. 8, 1975, p.5; July 10,
  1977, p.20; May 18, 1986, p.30; Nov. 5, 1995, p.22
New Yorker, Dec. 13, 1993, p.121
Newsweek, Nov. 24, 1975, p.120
Publishers Weekly, July 26, 1991, p.11
School Library Journal, July 1990, p.23
Top of the News, Winter 1983, p.199
VOYA, Oct. 1984, p.211

Washington Post Book World, Sep. 5, 1993, p.1
Wilson Library Bulletin, Mar. 1981, p.530

Online Articles

http://authors4teens.com
  (*Authors4Teens.com*, "Robert Lipsyte Interview," Aug. 30, 2001)
http://www.carr.lib.md.us/mae/lipsyte/lipsyte.htm
  Mona Kerby's The Author Corner, "Robert Lipsyte Biography," May 15,
  2001)

Online Database

Biography Resource Center, 2002, articles reproduced from *Contemporary Authors Online, 2001; St. James Guide to Young Adult Writers, 1999*

ADDRESS

HarperCollins Children's Books
1350 Avenue of the Americas
New York, NY 10019

Lillian Morrison 1917-
American Poet, Anthologist, and Librarian
Author and Editor of Children's Poetry Collections

BIRTH

Lillian Morrison was born on October 27, 1917, in Jersey City, New Jersey. She is the daughter of William and Rebecca (Nehamkin) Morrison. Her family included one older sister and one younger brother.

YOUTH

Morrison grew up in a modest but happy home environment. "My parents were immigrants from Russia and had to struggle to make a living for our family," she recalled. "Because we moved often, depending on our economic fortunes, I went to six different elementary schools. I liked some schools more than others, but I didn't mind all the moving. It meant a new block, a new neighborhood to explore."

Indeed, Morrison was a curious, outgoing child who loved to exercise both her body and mind. "Mine was a city childhood, and our playground was the street," she once said. "We jumped rope, roller-skated, took turns racing around the block, timing each other, and played almost every kind of ball game — bounce ball, stoop ball, box ball, stick ball. We saved picture cards of baseball players and boxers and went to movies on Saturday afternoons." She even used to go to boxing matches with her brother, with whom she had a close relationship. "As a child I lived for two years in an apartment house where there was a boxing ring in the basement and watched the fights that took place there. Being with my brother a great deal helped me to become acquainted with sports."

> **"Mine was a city childhood, and our playground was the street. We jumped rope, roller-skated, took turns racing around the block, timing each other, and played almost every kind of ball game — bounce ball, stoop ball, box ball, stick ball. We saved picture cards of baseball players and boxers and went to movies on Saturday afternoons."**

Morrison did not write poetry as a child, but she enjoyed singing and shouting playground rhymes and chants with her friends. She also liked to relax by curling up with an interesting book. She credits this early interest in literature to her parents. "My father was an avid reader and would often quote Shakespeare and read [Edgar Allen] Poe's "The Raven" and "The Bells" to us," Morrison explained. "It was from my mother, on the other hand, that I got my 'folk sense,' what with her rich store of catchy proverbs, folk sayings, and songs from the old country."

EDUCATION

Morrison graduated from high school in the mid-1930s. She then used academic scholarships and money earned from waitressing to put herself through Douglass College at Rutgers University. After earning a bachelor's degree in mathematics from Douglass in 1938, she enrolled at the School

The New York Public Library.

of Library Service at Columbia University. She earned her graduate degree from Columbia in 1942.

CAREER HIGHLIGHTS

Lillian Morrison has enjoyed rewarding careers as a librarian, a writer, and an editor of poetry and folk rhymes for children. She worked in the public libraries of New York City for four decades, during which time she became one of the city's leading voices for the library's youth services. But Morrison is even better known for her work as a poet and anthologist of teen-oriented poems that celebrate sports, women, and American folklore. In fact, the anthologies of poetry that Morrison has compiled over the years, including *Yours Till Niagara Falls* and *Sprints and Distances*, are regarded as classics of children's literature.

Finding a Home in New York's Libraries

Morrison's distinguished career as a librarian began with a lucky encounter. She was strolling through New York City one day in 1942 when she met a friend who told her that there was a job opening at the New York Public Library on 42nd Street. "I went in, applied, and got a job as a filer," recalled Morrison. "I loved it. It was quite a relief from my work in the statistical department at Bamberger's, a large department store in

Newark, New Jersey. I was surrounded by books. The whole world opened up to me. I knew I was in heaven!"

Shortly after joining the library staff, Morrison developed a keen interest in poetry. She took home all sorts of poetry collections for pleasure reading, and even began to try her own hand at writing verse. Before long, she found that writing poetry gave her a rare sort of pleasure. "In writing, I often experienced the same feelings of excitement that I had as a child running fast, jumping high, or catching a difficult fly ball," she explained. "There was the same aiming for perfection, the attempt to do something skillful and graceful."

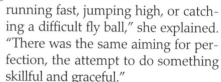

Morrison's career as a librarian began with a lucky encounter, when a friend told her about a job opening at the New York Public Library. "I went in, applied, and got a job as a filer. I loved it. It was quite a relief from my work in the statistical department at Bamberger's, a large department store in Newark, New Jersey. I was surrounded by books. The whole world opened up to me. I knew I was in heaven!"

As the years passed by, Morrison worked in libraries all around the city of New York. She particularly enjoyed organizing reading and activity programs for children and teenagers. In 1952, she became the assistant coordinator of young adult services for the entire New York City public library system, a position she would hold for 16 years. In 1968 she was promoted to head coordinator of the system's young adult service programs. She served the city's children and teens in that capacity for the next 15 years, until her retirement in 1982.

Morrison's work with young people across New York City also became the foundation for her career as a writer and collector of children's poetry and rhymes. She recalled that during her first years as an assistant librarian, many children possessed "autograph albums." These were notebooks in which the owner's friends, relatives, and teachers would write affectionate greetings, funny rhymes, and other messages. "Children would bring me their autograph albums to sign," Morrison remembered. "I used to love to write in their books and became curious as to what others had written. I began to collect the comments for fun—I'm a collector from way back!—realizing that the simple messages and the funny verses were actually a form of folklore that could be traced back to the Elizabethan era [the period from 1558 to 1603 in England,

when Queen Elizabeth I reigned over the country]. I had thousands of these sayings, each written on a 3x5 inch card and stored in shoeboxes. Finally I approached several publishing houses with the idea of doing a compilation of the verses."

A Leading Anthologist of Children's Poetry

Morrison's ambition to create an anthology of entertaining verses and rhymes was realized in the late 1940s, when the Crowell Publishing Company agreed to publish the book. In 1950 the collection—called *Yours Till Niagara Falls*—was published. As it turned out, this book proved to be only the first of numerous poetry collections compiled by Morrison that were published by Crowell.

Morrison was delighted with the strong reception that *Yours Till Niagara Falls* received. Convinced that the "vitality and fun in folk rhymes . . . corresponded to these [same] qualities in the children" that she encountered every day at the library, she decided to organize other collections of verse for children. In 1953 she published *Black Within and Red Without: A Book of Riddles*. Years later, Morrison explained that she selected each entry in the book because it had "some feeling of myth or mystery or some catchy quality of rhyme or rhythm." Two years later, she released *A Dillar, A Dollar: Rhymes and Songs for the Ten O'Clock Scholar,* a lighthearted collection of folk sayings about school arranged by school subject. And in 1958 she collected a series of wishes, spells, and folklore set to rhyme under the title *Touch Blue.*

One of Morrison's favorite collections of children's poetry and rhymes was her *Sprints and Distances: Sports in Poetry and the Poetry in Sport.* This book, which she said "grew out of my own love of sports," was released in 1965, nearly ten years after she first began working on it. The anthology features verses praising the virtues of nearly every kind of sport and athletic endeavor, and it includes selections from many different eras and places in human history.

——— " ———

"In writing, I often experienced the same feelings of excitement that I had as a child running fast, jumping high, or catching a difficult fly ball. There was the same aiming for perfection, the attempt to do something skillful and graceful."

——— " ———

Sprints and Distances further solidified Morrison's reputation as a national expert on poetry and American folklore. In fact, her abilities were so widely recognized that she was approached by a number of publishers involved in poetry. She served as the general editor of the Crowell Publishing Company's "Poets Series" from 1964 to 1974, and worked as poetry editor of the *Film Library Quarterly* from 1968 to 1975.

A Respected Children's Poet

Despite Morrison's many responsibilities as a librarian administrator and anthologist of children's poetry, she still found time to write original works of poetry aimed at young adult audiences. In 1967 she published her first original collection of poems, titled *Ghosts of Jersey City.* One year later, she and co-author Jean Boudin released *Miranda's Music,* a collection of poems written especially for teenage girls.

Both of these collections received a warm welcome, but Morrison's most successful books of original poetry were inspired by her lifelong love of sports. In 1977 she published *The Side Walk Racer, and Other Poems of Sports and Motion.* This collection was notable not only for its joyful characterizations of sports and outdoor activities, but also for its inclusion of several poems celebrating the athletic abilities of women and girls. "These poems are rooted in positive experiences of childhood," observed Lilian Moore in *Horn Book Magazine.*

According to Morrison, *The Side Walk Racer* reflected her feeling that writing poetry conjured up feelings of motion and movement. "Body movement seems to be involved," she said. "I am drawn to athletes, dancers, drummers, jazz musicians, who transcend misery and frustration and symbolize for us something joyous, ordered, and possible in life."

In the 1980s and 1990s, Morrison continued to explore a range of subject areas in her poetry. In 1981, for example, she published a collection of original works about science-related topics in *Overheard in a Bubble Chamber and Other Science Poems.* In 1997, meanwhile, she compiled a book of happy

children's poems about food, called *I Scream, You Scream: A Feast of Food Rhymes*.

But Morrison returned to the subjects of sports and the wonderful athletic capacity of the human body in other poetry collections. In 1985, for instance, she wrote a series of original poems titled *The Break Dance Kids*. In this children's book, which also features colorful illustrations, Morrison celebrates young people's ability to dance, run, and jump with joy. "[Morrison's collection covers] an impressive range of poetic types, forms, and content appropriate for readers of all ages who, once out of their armchairs and away from their desks, can make the poems come alive," claimed a review in *Voice of Youth Advocates*.

Three years later, Morrison followed up with *Rhythm Road: Poems to Move To*. This collection, which featured poets ranging from Edgar Allan Poe to John Updike, was named one of the American Library Association's Best Books for Young Adults for 1988. "The richly worded poems [in *Rhythm Road*] sing and capture the imagination with clear images and patterns of sound that reverberate in the mind," according to *Children's Books and Their Creators*.

Morrison also compiled several poetry collections devoted to a single sport. In these works — the baseball-themed *At the Crack of the Bat* (1992) and *Slam Dunks: Basketball Poems* (1994) — she selected poems that emphasized the sounds of language as well as those that gave colorful descriptions

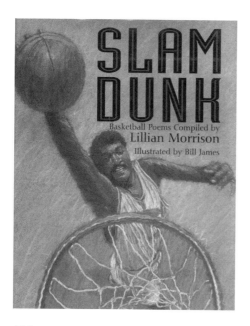

of athletes at play. In addition, she added some of her own poems about baseball and basketball that reflected her belief in the basic purity of the games. As with her earlier books, these two collections received a warm reception from readers. "Varied in style, some of the poems are tributes to superstars, some reflect the experience of playing the game, and others celebrate the swish of ball through net," said *Booklist* in a review of *Slam Dunks*. "[Morrison's book is] a choice collection for those who find poetry in basketball, but don't expect to find basketball in poetry."

Recent Works

In 2001 Morrison published an entire book of her own original sports-related poems for children, called *Way to Go! Sports Poems*. Many reviewers praised the author, as in this comment from *Childhood Education*: "Morrison's excellent style of writing, her precise choice of words, and her passion for sports are evident in this fun-to-read book." And *School Library Journal* described the title as "a fine blend of poetry and art that celebrates the joy and excitement of sports."

Still, Morrison has continued to show throughout her career that she has other interests besides athletics. In 1992 she surprised some

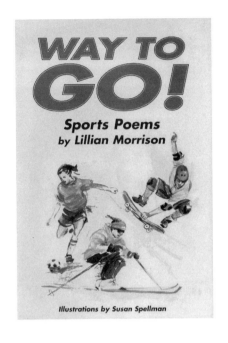

Illustrations by Susan Spellman

readers with *Whistling the Morning In,* a collection of original poems about nature "that greet the day and whatever the day brings," wrote Lilian Moore in *Horn Book Magazine*. "We may not think of Lillian Morrison as a 'nature' poet, but it is immediately clear that these new poems are vintage Morrison. The style is familiar—muscular, intimate, and celebratory." More recently, Morrison returned to the subject of women and their potential for doing great things. In *More Spice than Sugar: Poems about Feisty Females* (2001), Morrison gathered together a collection of poems that discuss issues of female identity and celebrate women's triumphs in the worlds of sports and human rights. "This lively anthology includes many contemporary children's poets as well as some classic adult writers," noted *School Library Journal*. "These poems are accessible, inspiring, and challenging."

HOME AND FAMILY

Morrison, a longtime resident of New York, never married and has no children.

HOBBIES AND OTHER INTERESTS

Morrison is a lifelong fan of jazz music. She also loves to travel, and continues to enjoy following sports of all kinds.

WRITINGS

Poetry Collections Written by Morrison

The Ghosts of Jersey City and Other Poems, 1967
Miranda's Music, 1968 (with Jean Boudin)
The Sidewalk Racer, and Other Poems of Sports and Motion, 1977
Who Would Marry a Mineral? 1978
The Break Dance Kids, 1985

Whistling the Morning In: New Poems, 1992
Way to Go! Sports Poems, 2001

Morrison has also contributed poems to many periodicals, including *Prairie Schooner, Images, Sports Illustrated, Atlantic Monthly,* and *Poetry Northwest.*

Poetry Collections Compiled by Morrison

Yours Till Niagara Falls, 1950
Black Within and Red Without: A Book of Riddles, 1953
A Dillar, A Dollar: Rhymes and Songs for the Ten O'Clock Scholar, 1955
Touch Blue: Signs and Spells, Love Charms and Chants, Auguries and Old Beliefs, in Rhyme, 1958
Remember Me When This You See: A New Collection of Autograph Verses, 1961
Sprints and Distances: Sports in Poetry and the Poetry in Sport, 1965
Best Wishes, Amen, 1974
Rhythm Road: An Anthology of Poems to Move To, 1988
At the Crack of the Bat: Baseball Poems, 1992
Slam Dunk: Basketball Poems, 1994
I Scream, You Scream: A Feast of Food Rhymes, 1997
More Spice than Sugar: Poems about Feisty Females, 2001

HONORS AND AWARDS

Notable Book (American Library Association): 1965, for *Sprints and Distances*; 1988 for *Rhythm Road*
American Ambassador Book (English Speaking Union): 1967, for *The Ghosts of Jersey City*
Grolier Award (American Library Association): 1987, awarded to a librarian whose "unusual contribution to the stimulation and guidance of reading by children and young people" exemplifies outstanding achievement in the profession
Best Book for Young Adults (American Library Association): 1988, for *Rhythm Road*

FURTHER READING

Books

Anthology of Children's Literature, 4th rev. ed., 1970
Children's Books and Their Creators, 1995
Contemporary Authors, New Revision Series, Vol. 7, 1982; Vol. 22, 1988
Continuum Encyclopedia of Children's Literature, 2001

Hopkins, Lee Bennett. *Books Are by People,* 1969
Sixth Book of Junior Authors and Illustrators, 1989
Something About the Author, Vol. 3, 1972; Vol. 108, 2000

Periodicals

Booklist, Oct. 1, 1995, p.311; Nov. 15, 1997, p.556; Mar. 15, 2001, p.1392
Book Report, Jan./Feb. 2002, p.67
Childhood Education, Spring 2002, p.171
Horn Book Magazine, May/June 1993, p.303
School Library Journal, Nov. 1995, p.92; Mar. 2001, p.274; Oct. 2001, p.189
Voice of Youth Advocates, Oct. 1985, p.278; June 1988, p.103

Online Database

Biography Resource Center, 2002; article reproduced from *Contemporary Authors Online,* 2002

ADDRESS

Boyds Mills Press
815 Church Street
Honesdale, PA 18431

WORLD WIDE WEB SITE

http://www.boydsmillspress.com/authors.tpl?command=showpage&
authorid=0768

Linda Sue Park 1960-
American Novelist for Children and Young Adults
Winner of the 2002 Newbery Medal for *A Single Shard*

BIRTH

Linda Sue Park was born on March 25, 1960, in Urbana, Illinois. Her parents were Eung Won Ed Park, a computer analyst, and Susie Kim Park, a teacher. Both of her parents had grown up in Korea. But their country underwent tremendous upheaval and destruction during the Korean War, and in the early 1950s they immigrated to the United States in search of a better life. They ultimately settled in Illinois, where Linda Sue and her two younger siblings, Fred and Julie, were raised.

YOUTH

For as long as she can remember, Park has loved using her imagination to create stories. "[I started] scribbling stories and poems when I was in kindergarten," she recalls. This early enthusiasm for writing was matched only by her enjoyment of reading. "I was a maniacal reader," she acknowledges. "It was by far my favorite activity. I read indiscriminately—from series like *Nancy Drew* and *Trixie Belden* to the award winners and everything in between."

Both of Park's parents were very supportive of their young child's passion for literature. They praised her early writing efforts, and Park recalls that her father "took me to the library every two weeks without fail. Because he didn't know much about American children's books himself, he just took me there to learn." Park appreciated her regular visits to the library so much that when a children's magazine called *Trailblazer* accepted one of her poems for publication, the little nine-year-old gave the one-dollar check she received as payment to her father as a gift. Eung Won was so proud of his daughter's achievement —and delighted with her generosity —that he framed the check and displayed it in their home.

"I was a maniacal reader. It was by far my favorite activity. I read indiscriminately—from series like **Nancy Drew** *and* **Trixie Belden** *to the award winners and everything in between."*

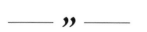

Park grew up not knowing much about her Korean heritage. Living in Illinois, her parents had wanted to fit in with other people in their neighborhood, so they only spoke English in their household. They also had not provided many details to their children about growing up in Korea. Then at age 11, Park visited her grandparents in Korea for the first time. The vacation was a fascinating experience, for it marked her first significant exposure to her Korean heritage. After arriving in Korea, Park strode through crowds of people in which Korean was the only language she heard, and unfamiliar sights, sounds, and smells danced all around her. By the time she returned to her familiar Illinois home, an enduring interest in Korean culture and history had taken root in her mind.

Throughout her teen years, Park spent much of her free time composing stories and poems or reading books. For the most part, she remained happy to use the library as her primary source of reading pleasure. But she admitted that once in a while, she wished that she could afford to amass a book collection of her own that would include all her favorite tales. "I have one vivid memory of being about 12 years old and going to baby-sit for a little girl who lived in the neighborhood, and being absolutely amazed at her bookshelf," she recalls. "She owned hundreds of books, what looked to me like every book I'd ever had from the library. Of course, I knew on one level that people could own books, but it never really sank in until I saw this little girl's room. Growing up, I owned almost no books, and I can really remember the ones I owned because I had so few. I read everything, but it was always from the library."

EDUCATION

Park attended elementary and high school in the Urbana public school system, and she credits several of her teachers with nurturing her love for reading and writing. She was a fine student who showed particular promise in English. After graduating from high school, Park enrolled at prestigious Stanford University in Palo Alto, California.

While at Stanford, Park competed in gymnastics and studied English. "Every school or 'career' decision I've made has revolved around reading and writing," she acknowledged. "I majored in English so I could read and write all the time in college." She graduated from Stanford in 1981 with a bachelor's degree in English. She then moved to Chicago, where she wrote a company newsletter for Standard Oil. "I don't remember a conscious decision to become a writer," she later admitted. "It was the only thing besides reading that I really wanted to do—and one of the few things I was any good at!"

As it turned out, however, Park only stayed in Chicago for a short time. A few months after her arrival, she met an Irish newspaper reporter named Ben Dobbin, and they became romantically involved. When Dobbin's work visa expired in 1983, Park accompanied him back to Ireland. They settled in Dublin, where she enrolled at Trinity College. One year later, in 1984, she graduated with a higher diploma in Anglo-Irish literature. That same year, she and Dobbin were married.

The newlyweds moved to London, where Park kept a busy schedule for the next several years. She continued her education, earning a master's degree from London's Birkbeck College in 1988. But during this same time, she wrote occasional restaurant reviews for London newspapers and taught "English as a Second Language" (ESL) courses—language classes for immigrants who did not speak English as their native language. She also established herself as a talented writer of poetry for adults, publishing poems in literary magazines like *Poetry Ireland,* the *Irish Times,* and the *Avatar Review.* Finally, Park and her husband started a family, welcoming both a son and daughter into the world in the late 1980s.

> *"I have been writing all my life, but only after I had children of my own did I feel the desire to explore my [Korean] ethnic heritage through writing. The fascinating discoveries I made have resulted in several books for young people. I continue to write poetry and fiction for adults as well, but because books were so important to me during my childhood, my work in children's literature holds special importance in my heart."*

CAREER HIGHLIGHTS

The joys and responsibilities of motherhood gradually changed Park's outlook on writing. "I have been writing all my life, but only after I had children of my own did I feel the desire to explore my [Korean] ethnic heritage through writing," she said. "The fascinating discoveries I made have resulted in several books for young people. I continue to write poetry and fiction for adults as well, but because books were so important to me during my childhood, my work in children's literature holds special importance in my heart." But the author is not the only one who treasures her work. Park's novels for young people—*Seesaw Girl, The Kite Fighters, When My Name Was Keoko,* and the 2002 John Newbery Medal Winner, *A Single Shard*—are admired and beloved by young and old for their fascinating glimpses into Korean history and their graceful exploration of universal human emotions like love, fear, envy, and hope.

Returning to America

Park's decision to write stories based on events and periods in Korean history did not occur immediately, however. In 1990 she and Dobbin returned to the United States when he received a work transfer to New York City. For the first few years after her return to America, Park kept herself busy raising her young children and teaching English as a second language in the New York City area.

As Park's children grew older, however, she felt increasingly drawn to the idea of exploring her Korean heritage. "[My] children are half-Korean, but I didn't know much about Korean culture. I wanted to learn more about the culture for them and for myself as well. So I started doing some research and it turned out to be a wonderful, really fascinating culture."

Seesaw Girl

Park's growing interest in Korean history eventually led her to consider writing a young adult novel set during an earlier era of Korean life. Once she decided to try her hand at such a tale, she drew on one of her childhood reading experiences for inspiration. As she started writing her first novel, *Seesaw Girl*, she was particularly inspired by *Tales of a Korean Grandmother*, by Frances Carpenter. "When I was ten years old, I read in [*Tales of a Korean Grandmother*] how girls in aristocratic families were almost never allowed to leave their homes. This made such an impression on me that 27 years later, it became the basis of *Seesaw Girl*. I wanted to write a story about how a girl with a lot of curiosity might cope in those conditions."

Park began writing *Seesaw Girl* in 1997, and two years later it became the first of her books for young people. Set in 17th-century Korea, the novel tells the story of 12-year-old Jade Blossom. Jade is a member of a wealthy family with connections to the kingdom's royal family. She lives in a huge, fortress-like compound, and all her physical needs are taken care of by servants. But Jade is an adventurous and curious girl who dislikes some aspects of her pampered life. For example, Korean traditions of the 17th-century called for girls from her social background to be totally shielded from the outside world. This means that Jade is not allowed to venture outside the compound's walls until her wedding day. As the novel progresses, however, Jade's hunger to explore the world beyond the fortress walls becomes so great that she sneaks out of the compound. During her brief adventure she encounters scenes of terrible poverty and hunger, as well as visions of great beauty and wonder. After reluctantly returning to the compound, Jade then makes a large seesaw that enables her to rise high in the air and see the outside world once again.

Seesaw Girl drew strong praise from many reviewers. The reviewer for *Booklist* applauded the author's "descriptive, engaging prose" and noted that Jade's eye-opening adventure shows her that "her home's high walls offer both shelter and imprisonment." *School Library Journal*, meanwhile, added that "like Jade's stand-up seesaw, Park's novel offers readers a brief but enticing glimpse at another time and place."

"[My] children are half-Korean, but I didn't know much about Korean culture. I wanted to learn more about the culture for them and for myself as well. So I started doing some research and it turned out to be a wonderful, really fascinating culture."

The Kite Fighters

Park based her second young adult (YA) novel on the traditional Korean sport of "kite fighting," in which competitors seek to cut other kites free of their strings while simultaneously remaining in a designated area of air space. One of her chief research sources for this book was her own father, who had actively participated in the sport of kite fighting as a youth. In fact, Park even arranged to have her father draw the chapter heading decorations for the book.

Set in 1473 in Seoul, Korea, *The Kite Fighters* (2000) features two brothers named Kee-sup and Young-sup who are one of the city's finest kite-flying teams. Kee-sup is an enormously talented designer and builder of kites, while his younger brother Young-sup is one of the finest kite fliers in the city. One day the young king of Korea approaches them and asks them to represent him in an important kite-fighting competition. Honored at the opportunity to represent their king, Kee-sup builds a magnificent kite that is decorated like a dragon and Young-sup devotes long hours to learning how to fly it. But the brothers' close relationship is threatened when their father insists that they follow a Korean tradition that calls for the eldest son to represent his family in important community events. According to their father, this tradition means that Young-sup must stand aside and let his older brother fly the kite, even though he is less skilled at kite-flying.

As with Park's first novel, *The Kite Fighters* drew praise from reviewers. "Though the story is set in medieval times, the brothers have many of the same issues facing siblings today," noted *School Library Journal*. "They play and argue, they compete for their father's attention, and eventually develop a greater understanding of one another. The author has drawn her characters with a sure touch, creating two very different boys struggling to figure out who they are. With ease and grace, Park brings these long-ago children to life."

A Single Shard

Park was delighted with the response to her first two books. Moreover, her efforts on those two works provided her with the foundation for her next novel. "In doing my research on Korea for

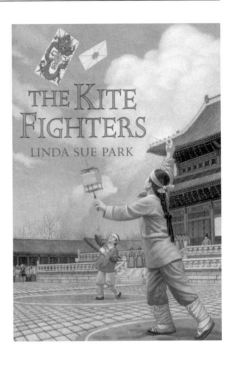

my first two books, I kept coming upon the fact that in the 11th and 12th centuries Korean pottery was considered the finest in the world—better even than China's," she explained. "This is what first interested me. I liked the idea that a tiny country like Korea could be the best in the world at something."

Park eventually used this slice of Korea's past as the basis for her 2001 novel *A Single Shard*. This book for young adults is set in Korea in the 12th century, a time of great artistic expression but also an era in which many Koreans lived in terrible hunger and poverty. The main character in the story is an orphan boy named Tree-ear. As the novel begins, he lives under a bridge with Crane-Man, a wise but poor old straw weaver. One day while out scrounging for food, Tree-ear draws near an area of the village where the finest potterymakers practice their trade. When he accidentally drops a piece of pottery created by Min, the finest artisan in the village, he agrees to pay off the cost of the pot by working for Min as an apprentice, a type of assistant. But Tree-ear also works at Min's shop every day because he wants to learn how to make beautiful pottery of his own. As time passes, the gruff Min gives greater responsibilities to the boy until one day, he asks Tree-ear to take the two precious pots to the king. Tree-ear sets out on his journey with a glad heart, but he encounters robbers and other dangers. These obstacles eventually reduce his

package to a single shard from one of the pots. But Tree-ear is so committed to carrying out his mission that he continues on and delivers the fragment to the king.

A Single Shard garnered Park her most flattering reviews yet. *Kirkus Reviews* described the book as a "timeless jewel" that "conveys a time and place far away and long ago, but with a simplicity and immediacy that is both graceful and unpretentious." *Booklist* promised readers that they would "feel the hunger and cold that Tree-ear experiences, as well as his shame, fear, gratitude, and love." The *Sacramento Bee,* meanwhile, declared that "Park's smooth writing, lively dialogue, and authentic scenes flow with the universal emotions of love, pride, and shame."

Praise and admiration for *A Single Shard* jumped another notch a few months later, when it received the prestigious 2002 John Newbery Medal from the American Library Association. This honor is given out every year to the most distinguished children's book published in the United States in the previous year. Park was stunned by the announcement. She later said that "it was like having a truck dropped on my head! It was a complete shock, a wonderful one though." But Kathleen Odean, the chairperson of the Newbery Medal selection committee, insisted that Park's book deserved the honor: "Tree-ear's determination and bravery in pursuing his dream of becoming a potter takes readers on a literary journey that demonstrates how courage, honor, and perseverance can overcome great odds and bring great happiness. Park effectively conveys 12th-century Korea in this masterful piece of historical fiction."

After winning the Newbery Medal, Park said that "it was like having a truck dropped on my head! It was a complete shock, a wonderful one though."

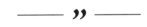

Newbery Medal Brings Fame and Excitement

In June 2002 the American Library Association formally awarded the Newbery Medal to Park at a special ceremony. After accepting the award, she surprised the audience by announcing that she intended to give it to her father. She explained that the medal was to thank him for all the times he had taken her to the library, the place where her lifelong love for reading and writing had blossomed.

Since winning the Newbery Medal, Park admits that her life has changed. For example, the award made her an instant celebrity in Korea. "The Newbery news has been in many Korean newspapers and on Korean television," she confirmed in 2002. "There will be Korean translations of my books, and I will probably be visiting Korea later this year! I received many messages of congratulations from Koreans—complete strangers—who wrote to tell me they were proud that a Korean-American had won this award. I even received a wonderful letter from Korea's First Lady! This was all very thrilling and humbling." Many people wrote to tell her how much her book meant to them and how proud they were that a book set in Korea and written by a Korean-American won the award. Park was also happy that many young people of Asian heritage will be able to see them-selves reflected in her book and will feel included in American society and literature.

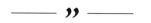

> *Park says that winning the Newbery Medal has made it easier for her to get out of bed in the morning. "It has just been so wonder-ful," she marveled. "I tell kids on my school visits that it's like, you know how you feel special on your birthday? You just know when you wake up that it's going to be an exciting day? Well, that's what it feels like every morning since I've won the Newbery."*

According to Park, winning the New-bery Medal has even made it easier for her to get out of bed in the morning. "It has just been so wonderful," she marveled. "I tell kids on my school vis-its that it's like, you know how you feel special on your birthday? You just know when you wake up that it's going to be an exciting day? Well, that's what it feels like every morning since I've won the Newbery."

When My Name Was Keoko

Park's fourth book for young adults, *When My Name Was Keoko,* was re-leased in 2002, the same year she won the Newbery Medal. This novel takes place from 1940 to 1945 in Korea, a period during World War II when the country was occupied by Japanese military forces. The Japanese invaders suppressed Korean culture and subju-gated the Korean people. They forced Koreans to take Japanese names and study only Japanese history. They even forbade the use of the Korean lan-guage.

According to Park, both her parents had many dark memories of this peri-od of their lives. Both of them had been forced to live for years under these restrictions, and Keoko—the name used in the novel's title—had been the Japanese name that her mother adopted during these difficult years. "My parents told me almost no stories of World War II when I was growing up," recalled Park. "But once I decided to explore the topic and begin researching, I asked them about their experiences and they did start talking. And talking . . . and talking! . . . I asked why they had never told me any of this before, and they said that it had indeed been a difficult time. Once they were in America and settled into their lives here, they sort of wanted to forget all that. But I think it's important to share stories —the hard ones as well as the ones that make us laugh. Your past is a huge part of what makes you 'you,' and exploring the past can help you better understand the present and the future."

When My Name Was Keoko is told from the perspective of a ten-year-old Korean girl named Sun-hee and her 13-year-old brother, Tae-yul. Each chapter of the story alternates between these two characters, providing insights into how they feel about the frightening and frustrating world in which they now live. As the story progresses, Sun-hee, Tae-yul, and the other members of their family all fight to preserve their Korean heritage and their dignity under foreign rule. These rebellions take varying forms, from publishing an illegal newspaper to choosing a new family name that echoes the meaning of their original Korean name. Eventually, Japanese authorities become suspicious of one member of the family, leading Tae-yul to make a brave sacrifice.

Reviewers hailed *When My Name Was Keoko* as another excellent work for young adult audiences. *School Library Journal* described it as a "beautifully crafted and moving novel." Likewise, *Kirkus Reviews* declared that "this powerful and riveting tale of one close-knit, proud Korean family movingly addresses life-and-death issues of courage and collaboration, injustice, and death-defying determination in the face of totalitarian oppression."

Looking to the Future

Park intends to branch out into other areas of writing in the next several years. "I have five picture books that will be published over the next few years," she said. "The first is called *The Fire-Keeper's Son,* and is based on an episode from Korean history. . . . Hopefully that book will be out in 2003.

125

Also forthcoming are two fun rhyming picture books for very young children; a book about animal noises around the world; and a collection of poetry for elementary-school kids."

But Park seems intent on adding to her list of young adult novels, too, even though she admits that she only averages one novel idea a year. "There are of course innumerable things worthy of a novelist's attention, but for me it's a question of feeling utterly captivated by an idea," she explained. "I have to feel 'obsessed' about something to want to spend so much time writing and thinking about it. . . . Once I get an idea for a book, I 'have' to finish it — because I know another one isn't going to come along for a long time!"

> "There are of course innumerable things worthy of a novelist's attention, but for me it's a question of feeling utterly captivated by an idea. I have to feel 'obsessed' about something to want to spend so much time writing and thinking about it. . . . Once I get an idea for a book, I 'have' to finish it — because I know another one isn't going to come along for a long time!"

Writing is also enjoyable for Park because she likes the "building process" in writing a novel. "Putting the right scenes together into scenes, and putting those scenes together into a story with just the right pace and tension. It's so challenging — and so satisfying when you've done it," she said. Finally, Park enjoys writing because it gives her an opportunity to educate readers about a world previously unknown to them. "In the last couple of generations, our world has gotten dramatically smaller, and the popularity of the Web has accelerated that process," she pointed out. "A kid can now 'chat' with someone halfway around the world as easily as with the kid next door! So paradoxically, their worlds are getting bigger at the same time. They need to learn more about the world, about other places, their cultures and traditions. To me, this is the most wonderful part about writing stories set in diverse locales and times: the opportunity to explore how people are different and more importantly, how we are alike."

MARRIAGE AND FAMILY

Park married Ben Dobbin, a journalist, on September 8, 1984. They live in Rochester, New York, with their two children, Sean and Anna.

HOBBIES AND OTHER INTERESTS

Park enjoys cooking, reading, and watching movies. She is also an avid baseball and soccer fan, and she loves to test her knowledge of words with the crossword puzzles in the *New York Times*.

WRITINGS

Seesaw Girl, 1999
The Kite Fighters, 2000
A Single Shard, 2001
When My Name Was Keoko, 2002

Linda Sue Park has also published poetry for adults that has appeared in a wide variety of periodicals, including *Poetry Ireland, Irish Times, Perihelion, Octavo, Avatar Review,* and *Atlanta Review.*

HONORS AND AWARDS

100 Titles for Reading and Sharing (New York Public Library): 1999, for
    Seesaw Girl; 2001, for *A Single Shard*
Best of the Best List (Chicago Public Library): 2000, for *The Kite Fighters*
Notable Books for a Global Society Award: 2001, for *The Kite Fighters*
Best Books List (*School Library Journal*): 2001, for *A Single Shard*
John Newbery Medal (American Library Association): 2002, for *A Single Shard*

FURTHER READING

Books

Something About the Author, Vol. 127, 2002

Periodicals

Booklist, Sep. 1, 1999, p.134; Apr. 1, 2000, p.1477; Apr. 1, 2001, p.1483
Columbus (Ohio) Dispatch, Apr. 25, 2002, p.F8
Current Biography, June 2002
Horn Book Magazine, May 2000, p.319; July-Aug. 2002, pp.377 and 387
Kirkus Reviews, Jan. 15, 2001
Miami Herald, Mar. 9, 2002, p.E6
Publishers Weekly, Mar. 5, 2001, p.80; Jan. 28, 2002, p.136; Mar. 4, 2002, p.80
Sacramento (Calif.) Bee, Apr. 7, 2002, p.L1

School Library Journal, Sep. 1999, p.228; June 2000, p.152; May 2001, p.158; July 1, 2002, p.48
Washington Post, Feb. 21, 2002, p.C14

Online Articles

http://www.ala.org/alsc/newbery.html
   (*Newbery Medal Home Page,* undated)
http://www.cynthialeitichsmith.com/auth-illLindaSuePark.htm
   (*Cynthia Leitich Smith Children's Literary Resources,* "Interview with Children's Book Author Linda Sue Park," May 7, 2002)
http://www.timeforkids.com/TFK/park
   (*Time For Kids.com,* "Author Linda Sue Park," undated)

Online Database=

Biography Resource Center Online, 2002

ADDRESS

Clarion Books
215 Park Avenue South
New York, NY 10003

E-mail: lspark@lindasuepark.com

WORLD WIDE WEB SITE

http://www.lindasuepark.com

Pam Muñoz Ryan 1951-

American Writer of Books for Children and Young
Adults
Winner of the 2002 Pura Belpré Award for *Esperanza
Rising*

BIRTH

Pam Muñoz Ryan was born on December 25, 1951, in Bakersfield, California. Her maiden name was Pamela Bell, and her
married name is Ryan. Muñoz is a family name, taken from
her grandmother, Esperanza Ortega Muñoz, and her mother,
Esperanza Muñoz Bell (also called Hope). Her mother, Hope

Bell, worked as a librarian's assistant in a high school library, and her father, Don Bell, was a delivery man for a distribution company. Pam is the oldest child in her family, with two younger sisters, Sally and Linda, and 23 younger cousins on her mother's side.

Ryan's family originally came from Mexico, and she grew up speaking both English and Spanish, as she explains here. "My grandmother and grandfather came to the United States from Aguascalientes, Mexico, in the 1930s. They were very determined that their children (my mother, aunts, and uncles) learn and speak English so that they could compete and succeed in the United States. They all learned and spoke English within a few years of arriving. I was fortunate that my grandmother only spoke to me in Spanish! I think it gave me an appreciation for the rhythm of two languages."

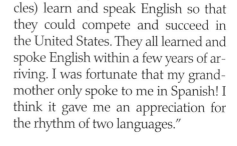

> *"Growing up, I spent many long, hot valley summers riding my bike to the library. The library became my favorite hang out because my family didn't have a swimming pool and the library was air-conditioned. That's how I got hooked on reading and books. . . . Today, I am a full-time writer and not much has changed. I still don't have a swimming pool and I still spend time at the library."*

YOUTH

Ryan was raised in Bakersfield, located in California's San Joaquin Valley. "I grew up with aunts, uncles, and grandparents nearby and consider myself truly American because my heritage is part Spanish, Mexican, Basque, Italian, and Oklahoman," she said. Surrounded by a large and gregarious extended family, Ryan recalls that "many of my childhood memories revolve around big, noisy family gatherings."

The world of literature caught Ryan's interest at an early age. "Growing up, I spent many long, hot valley summers riding my bike to the library," she said. "The library became my favorite hang out because my family didn't have a swimming pool and the library was air-conditioned. That's how I got hooked on reading and books. . . . Today, I am a full-time writer and not much has changed. I still don't have a swimming pool and I still spend time at the library." As Ryan grew older, she occasionally tried her hand at writing short stories and reporting on sports events for the Washington Junior High School newspaper, where she became the editor in eighth grade. But reading accounted for most of her involvement in literature during her youth.

EDUCATION

Ryan attended McKinley and Jefferson elementary schools, Washington Junior High, and Bakersfield High School. After earning her high school diploma in 1969, she enrolled at San Diego State University. She earned a bachelor's degree in Child Development in 1973. After that, she took several years off, to work, get married, and raise a family. She later returned to school, and in 1991 she earned a master's degree in Post-Secondary Education from San Diego State.

FIRST JOBS

After graduating from college in 1973, Ryan's first job was working as a volunteer for the Red Cross. She was the volunteer coordinator of play schools for refugee children at the relocation camp on Camp Pendleton, a U.S. military base north of San Diego. This was immediately following the Vietnam War, and many Vietnamese and Cambodians refugees who had come to the United States were staying at Camp Pendleton before being relocated in the U.S. Ryan worked with the children of these refugees in the play schools in the relocation camp.

After three months Ryan was ready for a change. "I knew that I wanted to work in a profession that had something to do with books, and so I became a teacher," she remembered. She then worked as a bilingual teacher in a Head Start program for three years. Head Start is a government-funded preschool program that is designed to give a "head start" to disadvantaged children. After several years as a bilingual teacher, teaching in both Spanish and English, Ryan was married and ready to start a family. For the next 12 years or so, she stayed home to take care of her children while they were young. Then, as her children grew up, she returned to school to get her master's degree and began to write.

CAREER HIGHLIGHTS

Today, Ryan is regarded as a talented writer of books for both younger and older children. Works in the latter category, such as *Riding Freedom* and *Amelia and Eleanor Go for a Ride*, have been warmly received by critics and readers alike. In addition, Ryan's novel *Esperanza Rising* was the 2002 winner of the Pure Belpré Award, which honors Latino children's authors who best portray the Latino cultural experience. But it was not until after she was 30 years old that Ryan even considered writing books for young people.

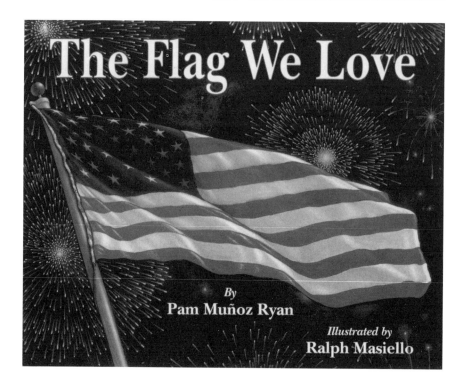

Becoming a Writer

In the early 1980s, Ryan was approached by a friend who encouraged her to use her writing talents to write a book. "That's when I discovered what I really wanted to do with my life," she later admitted. In the late 1980s, Ryan and Doris Jasinek—a fellow graduate of San Diego State University—co-authored three paperback books providing inspirational messages about parenting and family relations.

After completing her master's degree in education in 1991, Ryan worked as the director of early childhood education programs in nearby Encinitas for five years. But she had enjoyed working on the writing projects so much that she decided to write a book for children. Over time, this decision brought her a lot of frustration, for she spent several years writing children's stories before a publisher accepted one of them. But despite the rejections and other writing setbacks that she endured during that period, she never allowed discouragement to overwhelm her. Eventually, she had enough writing-related work to quit her job and become a full-time writer.

Ryan's first book for young children—*One Hundred Is a Family*—was published in 1994. It combined counting lessons with a celebration of the many types of families and friendships that exist in the world. *Booklist* called the book "comforting in that it presents and embraces a world in which every form of family is welcome," while *Publishers Weekly* remarked that "Ryan's first book rates high on jolliness if low on subtlety."

In 1996 Ryan published *The Flag We Love,* a book for young readers that honors the American flag and its symbolic value to the country. Ryan had written the book after visiting a supermarket where a flag had been draped over cases of beer as a promotion for Memorial Day. She was offended by the supermarket's disrespectful treatment of the flag. She wrote an indignant letter about the incident to the company president. When her own children wondered why she was upset, she went looking for a book on the flag for her own children—a picture book with big beautiful pictures that was simply written and evoked feelings and emotions—and she couldn't find one. "All of the picture books at that time were like social studies books,"she recalled. After *The Flag We Love* was published, reviewers agreed that Ryan had succeeded in communicating her intentions. "Strike up the band and prepare to salute," said *Publishers Weekly.* "This patriotic picture book unabashedly celebrates the Stars and Stripes."

Riding Freedom

Ryan's first book to receive widespread critical acclaim was *Riding Freedom* (1999), a story for middle school readers. It relates the true story of Charlotte "Charley" Darkey Parkhurst, an American woman in the 19th century who lived her life disguised as a man so she could be a stagecoach driver. She grew up in an orphanage, where she developed a deep love for horses. When the head of the or-

— " —

"The most wonderful thing about writing has been that I can 'try on' many lives that might be different from my own. When I write, I can be as strong as Charlotte in **Riding Freedom,** *and as determined as Eleanor Roosevelt, Amelia Earhart, and Marian Anderson. Or even as remarkable as Esperanza in* **Esperanza Rising.** *Part of the enchantment of writing (and reading, too) is the well of strengths, weaknesses, and idiosyncrasies that I can sample and then keep, discard, or consider for my characters, and ultimately for myself."*

— " —

133

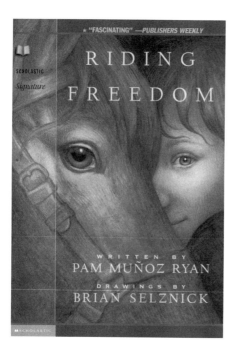

phanage refused to let her ride horses, she ran away and, disguised as a boy, secured a job as a stablehand. Over the ensuing years, she became one of the finest coachmen in New England. Parkhurst eventually moved to California. Still disguised as a man, she voted in the 1868 U.S. presidential election. That was 52 years before the 19th Amendment to the Constitution was ratified in 1920, granting women the right to vote. Historians believe that she was the first woman ever to vote in the United States.

Riding Freedom won several notable awards, including the Willa Cather Award and the California Young Reader Medal. It also garnered praise from readers and reviewers. *Publishers Weekly,* for example, stated that "with a pacing that moves along at a gallop, this is a skillful execution of a fascinating historical tale."

Writing about Two Famous Women

In the late 1990s Ryan decided to write a book about a brief but lively meeting between Amelia Earhart and Eleanor Roosevelt, two of the most famous women in American history. These two women are acclaimed for very different reasons, though. "In 1932, Amelia Earhart did what was then considered unthinkable," explained Ryan. "She flew [an airplane] solo across the Atlantic to demonstrate that 'women like to do such things, and can!'" Eleanor Roosevelt was the wife of U.S. President Franklin D. Roosevelt. She left her mark on the United States as an activist for women's and human rights. "She transformed the role of First Lady by becoming a commanding role model," said Ryan. "Her practical approach to issues gained her enormous respect. Many have said she was a woman ahead of her time. She would have said it was just common sense."

Ryan's 1999 book *Amelia and Eleanor Go for a Ride* was based on an actual event in April 1933, when Earhart and Roosevelt took a nighttime flight together over Washington, D.C. "For the purposes of this book, I sentimentally imagined Eleanor and Amelia in the cockpit, although the plane was actually flown by two of Easter Air Transport's regular pilots," admitted Ryan. "But Amelia did take the controls during part of the flight and Eleanor took a turn in the cockpit with the captain who explained the controls to her. When the plane took an unexpected dip, the reporters joked that Mrs. Roosevelt was flying the plane."

Critics widely praised *Amelia and Eleanor* as a fine book for young readers. *Publishers Weekly* called the story a "brief but compelling slice from the lives of two determined, outspoken and passionate women." A reviewer in the *Atlanta Journal and Constitution,* meanwhile, said that "all things considered, Ryan has beautifully blown the dust off this small episode in history. Here's a chance to recall two remarkable women who were ahead of their time and very much drawn to one another. This story soars as a celebration of friendship, spontaneity, woman power, and high adventure." *Amelia and Eleanor Go for a Ride* was eventually named an American Library Association Notable Book and an American Booksellers' Book of the Year finalist.

During the 1990s, Ryan received a lot of attention for her books targeted at older readers. But she also continues

——— **"** ———

Eleanor Roosevelt was the wife of U.S. President Franklin D. Roosevelt and an activist for women's and human rights.
"She transformed the role of First Lady by becoming a commanding role model. Her practical approach to issues gained her enormous respect. Many have said she was a woman ahead of her time. She would have said it was just common sense."

——— **"** ———

to write books for younger children. These books reflect not only the author's love for children, but also her ability to choose attractive subjects for little kids. In 1999, for example, she released *A Pinky Is a Baby Mouse,* which lists all the odd but true names that humans have given various baby animals. Ryan was inspired to write the book after learning that the baby animal name of a spiny anteater (the echindna) is called a puggle. Another of her books for young children, the 2002 picture book *Mud Is Cake,* builds on the fun that children can have with their imagination. "*Mud Is Cake* is a very sweet book that encourages children, and their parents, to engage in the magic of make-believe," stated the *New York Times.* "Ryan's lively rhymes and strong rhythms are easy and fun to read aloud."

Esperanza Rising

Ryan's best-known book is *Esperanza Rising,* a young adult novel that hit bookstores in 2000. The title character is a 13-year-old Mexican girl who grows up in a wealthy and privileged home in the 1930s. But her father's sudden death triggers a chain of events that forces Esperanza and her mother to leave Mexico and build a new life for themselves in California. They end up in the Mexican migrant-labor camps, home to the migrant workers who toil in California's farm fields. There they endure discrimination, poverty, and long days of difficult manual labor. But Esperanza eventually learns to stop grieving the loss of her past life and "embrace the riches that lay within her grasp: love, respect, and the chance to create a future of her own design," said *Reading Today.*

"What do I write about? I write about dreams, discoveries, and daring women. I write short stories about hard times, picture books about mice and beans, and novels about journeys. That's part of the enchantment of writing and creating characters—the variety."

Reviewers praised Ryan's novel as one of the year's finest books for young adults. "Ryan writes movingly in clear, poetic language that children will sink into," said *Booklist.* A review in *Reading Today* added that Ryan's "passionate" novel showed "an uncommon understanding of the plight of Mexican farm workers." And *Horn Book Magazine* added that over the course of the book, "Esperanza is transformed from a sheltered aristocrat into someone who can take care of herself and others. Although her material wealth is not restored in the end . . . she is rich in family, friends, and esperanza—the Spanish word for hope."

Esperanza Rising—which will be published in a Spanish-language version in the fall of 2002—also garnered several prestigious honors. The Smithsonian Institution and *Publishers Weekly* named it one of the top children's books of 2000, and it earned the Jane Addams Children's Book Award. In 2002 *Esperanza Rising* was also awarded the Pura Belpré Award, given out biennially by the American Library Association. It's presented to a Latino or Latina writer or illustrator whose work best portrays, affirms, and celebrates the Latino cultural experience in an outstanding work of literature for children and youth.

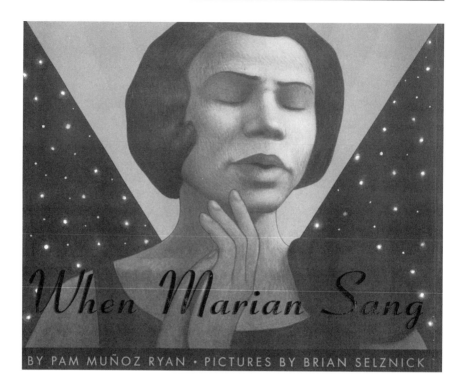

When Marian Sang

Ryan has since followed up *Esperanza Rising* with another book for older children. *When Marian Sang,* published in the fall of 2002, is an account of the life of Marian Anderson, an African-American woman who triumphed over racism to become one of the greatest singers in American history. In 1939—long before the civil rights movement helped black Americans gain equal rights in housing, employment, voting, and other areas—she gave a historic concert on the steps of the Lincoln Memorial in Washington, D.C. that drew an estimated audience of 75,000 people. The book shows her struggles, her courage, her dignity, and her strength. *When Marian Sang* is beautifully illustrated by Brian Selznick, with exquisitely detailed and elaborately designed pictures in sepia tones.

Early reviews of *When Marian Sang* seemed as positive as those for her other books, as in this review from *Publishers Weekly*, which called it "a picture book biography as understated and graceful as its subject, singer Marian Anderson." The reviewer continued, "Tracing the African-American diva from her beginnings as an eight-year-old church choir wonder ('the pride of South Philadelphia') through years of struggle to rise above the racism that would delay her debut with the Metropolitan Opera until she was 57, this book masterfully distills the events in the life of an extraordinary musician. Ryan's narrative smoothly integrates biographical details with lyrics from the gospel songs Anderson made famous." The writer for *Kirkus Reviews* agreed, saying "[Ryan acquaints young readers] with a time of social injustice when a person of color could not pursue a professional career in concert music and it was a act of personal courage to sing before racially mixed audiences. . . . Perfectly paced and perfectly pitched, this book never loses sight of the fact that Marian Anderson was both a world-class musician and a powerful symbol to her people."

Ryan encourages children to "daydream a little everyday and pretend often. Read lots of different kinds of books so you will know what is good and what is not-so-good literature. Write lots of different things: lists, stories, menus, notes. Lists are my personal favorites. Take time to pay attention to people, places, and things so you can soak in all the little details. That's a good beginning!"

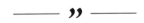

Keys to Ryan's Success

Ryan enjoys almost every aspect of her writing life. "The thing I like most about writing is that it is not boring," she explained. "Each project is different and although some novels take a year to write, they are still fun. The most wonderful thing about writing has been that I can 'try on' many lives that might be different from my own. When I write, I can be as strong as Charlotte in *Riding Freedom*, and as determined as Eleanor Roosevelt, Amelia Earhart, and Marian Anderson. Or even as remarkable as Esperanza in *Esperanza Rising*. Part of the enchantment of writing (and reading, too) is the well of strengths, weaknesses, and idiosyncrasies that I can sample and then keep, discard, or consider for my characters, and ultimately for myself." She also admits that by the time one of her story ideas blossoms into a book, she has rewritten it up to 30 times.

"What do I write about? I write about dreams, discoveries, and daring women. I write short stories about hard times, picture books about mice and beans, and novels about journeys. That's part of the enchantment of writing and creating characters — the variety."

Finally, Ryan encourages children to "daydream a little everyday and pretend often. Read lots of different kinds of books so you will know what is good and what is not-so-good literature. Write lots of different things: lists, stories, menus, notes. Lists are my personal favorites. Take time to pay attention to people, places, and things so you can soak in all the little details. That's a good beginning!"

MARRIAGE AND FAMILY

Ryan met her future husband, Jim Ryan, at a wedding they attended while still in college. They were married in 1975. They live in California, about 30 miles north of San Diego. There, they raised four children: two older daughters, Marcy and Annie, and identical twin sons, Matthew and Tyler, all of whom are now grown. They live only six blocks from the Pacific Ocean, so Ryan says that surfboards, beach towels, and wet suits are always lying around their home.

HOBBIES AND OTHER INTERESTS

Ryan's hobbies include reading, walking on the beach, and following her children's activities. She is also "very interested in Mexican culture and fascinated with its festivals," and has made a number of trips to Mexico. She loves to travel.

SELECTED WRITINGS

For Older Children

The Flag We Love, 1996 (illustrated by Ralph Masiell)
Riding Freedom, 1999 (illustrated by Brian Selznick)
Amelia and Eleanor Go for a Ride, 1999 (illustrated by Brian Selznick)
Esperanza Rising, 2000
When Marian Sang, 2002 (illustrated by Brian Selznick)

For Younger Children

One Hundred Is a Family, 1994 (illustrated by Ben Huang)
The Crayon Counting Book, 1996 (illustrated by Frank Mazzola, Jr.)
California Here We Come, 1997 (illustrated by Kay Salem)
A Pinky Is a Baby Mouse, 1997 (illustrated by Diane deGroat)
Armadillos Sleep in Dugouts, 1997 (illustrated by Diane deGroat)
Hello Ocean, 2001 (illustrated by Mark Astrella)

Mice and Beans, 2001 (illustrated by Joe Cepeda)
Mud Is Cake, 2002 (illustrated by David McPhail)
How Do You Raise a Raisin? 2002

For General Audiences

A Family Is a Circle of People Who Love You, 1988 (with Doris Jasinek)
How to Build a House of Hearts, 1988 (with Doris Jasinek)
Falling in Fun Again, 1990 (with Doris Jasinek)

HONORS AND AWARDS

Early Childhood News Director's Choice Award: 1997, for *The Flag We Love*
Notable Social Studies Trade Book (NCSS/CBC): 1997, for *The Flag We Love;* 2000, for *Amelia and Eleanor Go for a Ride*
Best Books (Bank Street): 1998, for *A Pinky Is a Baby Mouse*
Pick of the List (American Booksellers): 1998, for *A Pinky Is a Baby Mouse;* 1999, for *Amelia and Eleanor Go for a Ride*
Reading Magic Award (*Parenting Magazine*): 1999, for *Riding Freedom;* 1999, for *Amelia and Eleanor Go for a Ride*
Teachers' Choice Award: 1999, for *Riding Freedom;* 1999, for *Amelia and Eleanor Go for a Ride*
Willa Cather Award for Best Young Adult Novel: 1999, for *Riding Freedom*
Best Children's Books (New York Public Library): 1999, for *Amelia and Eleanor Go for a Ride*
Oppenheim Platinum Award: 2000, for *Amelia and Eleanor Go for a Ride*
Notable Children's Book (American Library Association): 2000, for *Amelia and Eleanor Go for a Ride*
Reading Magic Award (Parenting Magazine): 2000, for *Amelia and Eleanor Go for a Ride*
Best Books (Smithsonian Institution): 2000, for *Esperanza Rising*
Best Children's Books (*Publishers Weekly*): 2000, for *Esperanza Rising*
Top Ten Best Books for Young Adults (American Library Association): 2001, for *Esperanza Rising*
Jane Addams Children's Book Award (Women's International League for Peace and Freedom): 2001, for *Esperanza Rising*
Pura Belpré Award (American Library Association): 2002, for *Esperanza Rising*

FURTHER READING

Periodicals

Atlanta Journal and Constitution, Jan. 8, 2000, p.C3

Booklist, Nov. 1, 1994, p.509; Jan. 1, 1996, p.841; Jan. 1, 1998, p.814; Oct. 15, 1999, p.447; Dec. 1, 2000, p.708; Sep. 15, 2001, p.233; Nov. 1, 2001, p.493; Feb. 15, 2002, p.1022

Fresno (Calif.) Bee, Apr. 16, 1995, p.G8

Horn Book Magazine, Jan. 2001, p.96

Journal of Adolescent and Adult Literacy, Dec. 2001, p.334

Journal/Literacy: Classroom Connections, Vol. XX, 1995-96, p.23

Language Arts, Mar. 2002, p.356

Los Angeles Times, June 13, 1999, p.2; Nov. 19, 2000, p.12

New York Times, May 19, 2002, p.L32

Publishers Weekly, Nov. 7, 1994, p.78; Feb. 5, 1996, p.88; Feb. 2, 1998, p.91; Sep. 27, 1999, p.105; Feb. 18, 2002, p.94

Reading Today, Oct. 2000, p.32

School Library Journal, Oct. 2000, p.171; Apr. 2002, p.S10; May 2002, p.126

Online Articles

http://www.kconnect.com/pamryan.html
   (*The Kindergarten Connection,* "Pam Muñoz Ryan," undated)
http://www2.scholastic.com/teachers/authorsandbooks/authorstudies/
   authorstudies.jhtml (*Scholastic Authors and Books Homepage,*
   "Pam Muñoz Ryan's Biography," undated)

ADDRESS

Scholastic, Inc.
555 Broadway
New York, NY 10012

WORLD WIDE WEB SITE

http://www.pammunozryan.com

Lemony Snicket (Daniel Handler) 1970-

American Novelist
Author of the Popular Novels, *A Series of Unfortunate Events*

BIRTH

Daniel Handler was born in 1970 in San Francisco, California. His parents are Louis Handler, an accountant, and Sandra Handler, a dean of behavioral sciences at City College of San Francisco. He has one younger sister, Rebecca. Handler adopted the name Lemony Snicket several years ago, even before he began writing for kids. For the purposes of this profile, the author will be called Lemony Snicket, his chosen pen name.

———— " ————

"I didn't like stories where people ran off to summer camp and everybody just had a grand old time, or tried to join the soccer team. I think it's always depressing to me that there's so many books marketed for young boys who want to read that are about sports. . . . The idea that a bookworm boy would want to read about sports always cracked me up. That is exactly what the bookworm boys read books to get away from. They're hiding from the teacher at recess because they don't want to play kickball, and then the teacher is like, 'Here, read this book about a hockey team!'"

———— " ————

YOUTH

Snicket grew up in the San Francisco area in a peaceful neighborhood full of big houses with expansive lawns. A funny and imaginative child, he was popular with other kids his age. "He could see the humor in everything," recalled his mother. But he also was an observant and sensitive youngster. Sandra Handler remembers that as her son watched schoolyard bullies go unpunished for their actions and read stories detailing the cruelty and thoughtlessness that some people were capable of. Early on, he developed a "sense of unfairness in the world."

Snicket was drawn to literature as a young child, and by the time he was seven years old he was regularly writing stories of his own. Looking back at these early writing efforts, he says that he preferred to write stories "in which mysterious and creepy things happen." In fact, like many other young people, he often wished that he could be a "dark, mysterious person" to other people.

A self-described "sissy," Snicket did not like playing sports. He much preferred to spend his free time reading books by Roald Dahl, Edward Gorey, and Zilpha Keatley Snyder. All three of these authors wrote children's books that featured strange and creepy characters, spooky settings, and a sort of gloomy humor about life and death. "I didn't like stories where people ran off to summer camp and everybody just had a grand old time, or tried to join the soccer team," Snicket explained. "I think it's always depressing to me that there's so many books marketed for young boys who want to read that are about sports. . . . The idea that a bookworm boy would want to read about sports always cracked me up. That is exactly what the bookworm boys read books to get away from. They're hiding from the teacher at recess because they don't want to play kickball, and then the teacher is like, 'Here, read this book about a hockey team!'" He also admitted that he did not care for *The Lord of the Rings* or other fantasies that featured fire-breathing dragons and brave swordsmen. "I was never much of a fan of books in which people were casting spells," he said.

As Snicket grew older, his parents actively encouraged their son's interest in literature. "My parents were always very avid readers," he said, "and so I never got the sense that they really meant what they said when they said, 'You really ought to be outside playing baseball,' because neither of them are really athletic either. And so even though they would say that, it never really rang true. . . . One thing that they did that I just thought was fantastic was that they would read to me when I was very young and stop at a suspenseful moment. And then they would say, 'Well, it's now time for bed. And under no circumstances should you read with this light over here that we're placing near your bed. Under no circumstances should you turn this on and read [your book].' And then, of course, I would. And then the next day when the bookmark was in a different place in the book, they would read as if nothing had happened."

EDUCATION

Snicket attended San Francisco's prestigious Hoover Middle School and Lowell High School. He was an excellent and popular student who engaged in a wide variety of extracurricular activities, from editing the high school's literary magazine to playing tuba in the school band. In 1988 he was valedictorian of his graduating class, and his classmates voted him both "best personality" and "class clown."

Snicket attended college on the other side of the country from California, at Wesleyan University in Connecticut. Early in his stay at Wesleyan, he earned a Poets Prize from the Academy of American Poets. But during his time of study at the school he gradually moved away from poetry in favor of prose writing. In 1992 he graduated from Wesleyan with a bachelor's degree (B.A.) in American studies. Armed with an Olin Fellowship—a type of scholarship that includes a financial gift—he decided to write a novel.

In 1993 Snicket moved to San Francisco with his girlfriend, Lisa Brown, a fellow graduate of Wesleyan. For the next few years he divided his time between his novel and a part-time job as a comedy sketch writer for the

Daniel Handler

House of Blues Radio Hour, a San Francisco-based radio program that was broadcast by stations all around the country. In 1998 he and Brown were married, and in 2000 they relocated to Manhattan in New York City.

CAREER HIGHLIGHTS

Since embarking on his writing career, the author has completed two novels for adults that appear with his own name, Daniel Handler, on the cover. But he has achieved far greater fame as Lemony Snicket, the name he adopted for the children's book series collectively known as *A Series of Unfortunate Events.* In fact, his decision to narrate each book as the odd and mysterious Lemony Snicket has made him as famous with young readers as the three brave but unlucky Baudelaire children — Violet, Klaus, and Sunny — that are the central characters in the *Unfortunate Events* tales.

Breaking into Publishing

Snicket's first two novels were written for adults under his own name, Daniel Handler. In 1999 he published his first novel, *The Basic Eight,* about a popular clique of teenagers and their involvement in a murder. One year later, his book *Watch Your Mouth* hit bookstore shelves. In this second novel, a college student named Joseph becomes romantically involved with Cynthia, another student at his school. But when the couple decide to spend the summer with her family in Pittsburgh, he becomes puzzled by the family's strange ways and grows extremely uncomfortable with the sexual undertones of their interactions. Both books attracted kind words from reviewers, who described him as undeniably talented and witty. But neither novel became a major critical or popular success.

Even as he was completing *Watch Your Mouth,* however, he was also trying his hand at writing a book for children. He had never written a children's book before. But Susan Rich, an editor at a New York publishing company, convinced the author to make the attempt. "I knew we shared a similar sensibility about children's books, which I'd define as a resistance to fall into overly trodden paths of traditional stories, and a resistance to anything that is too sweet or patronizing or moralistic" she later explained. Before long, he became so excited about the project that he decided to write an entire series of books for kids, which became *A Series of Unfortunate Events*.

When Snicket agreed to make children his primary audience for his next writing effort, he did not bother to investigate the tone or style used by other contemporary writers of children's books. "I did very little reading of books that were meant for that age," he said. "I just tried to think of what I would have wanted to read when I was in third or fourth grade and write a story accordingly." With this in mind, he set about writing a tale that would capture the same feeling of dark fun and adventure that he had enjoyed in the books of Dahl, Gorey, and Snyder.

One of Snicket's first major decisions was to turn his main characters—three siblings—into orphans. "I think it was more just a basic fantasy that I think nearly every child and probably most adults have, which is, 'What if I were all alone in the world?'" He explained. "From that very first moment that you're maybe at the zoo and you take your mother's hand and you look up and it's not your mother, it's just some other tall person, and you suddenly have this sense of, 'What if I were alone? And what if no one was taking care of me?'"

The author also decided to draw the names of many of the series' characters from literature. For example, he gave the orphans the last name of Baudelaire, taken from Charles Baudelaire, a famous French poet of the 19th century. "The literary names are there mostly because I look forward to kids growing up and finding Baudelaire in the poetry anthology and having that be something else to be excited about,"

One of Snicket's first major decisions was to turn his main characters—three siblings—into orphans. "I think it was more just a basic fantasy that I think nearly every child and probably most adults have, which is, 'What if I were all alone in the world?'... From that very first moment that you're maybe at the zoo and you take your mother's hand and you look up and it's not your mother, it's just some other tall person, and you suddenly have this sense of, 'What if I were alone? And what if no one was taking care of me?'"

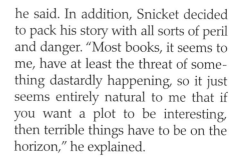

> "Most books, it seems to me, have at least the threat of something dastardly happening, so it just seems entirely natural to me that if you want a plot to be interesting, then terrible things have to be on the horizon."

he said. In addition, Snicket decided to pack his story with all sorts of peril and danger. "Most books, it seems to me, have at least the threat of something dastardly happening, so it just seems entirely natural to me that if you want a plot to be interesting, then terrible things have to be on the horizon," he explained.

The Mysterious Lemony Snicket

Finally, he decided to narrate each book in *A Series of Unfortunate Events* from the perspective of "Lemony Snicket," an imaginary author who relates the adventures of the Baudelaire children in a gloomy but entertaining way. "Lemony Snicket, this man who speaks directly to the reader and also who is tangentially involved in the story that he's telling, is really more a character," he said. "We just thought it would be fun to publish the books under the name of this character."

The author notes that he had actually been using the name Lemony Snicket for some time prior to the creation of the *Unfortunate Events* series. The name had been born a few years earlier, when he had been researching his adult novel *The Basic Eight*. "I needed to contact for research purposes some right-wing political organizations and religious groups, and I wanted material mailed to me, but I didn't want to be on their mailing list, for obvious reasons," he explained. "And so someone asked me, 'So what is your name?' And I opened my mouth and out popped the words, 'Lemony Snicket.' And so it became a joke among all of my friends. We would write letters to the newspaper and sign them Lemony Snicket . . . and reserve tables in restaurants under the [name] Lemony Snicket and all sorts of things like that."

In 1999 Snicket completed and published *The Bad Beginning*, the first book in *A Series of Unfortunate Events*. On the very first page, the author—writing as Lemony Snicket, of course—issued a humorous warning that the book was not like other children's books:

"If you are interested in stories with happy endings, you would be better off reading some other book. In this book, not only is there no happy ending, there is no happy beginning and very few happy things in the middle. This is because not very many happy things happened in the lives of the three Baudelaire youngsters. Violet, Klaus, and Sunny Baudelaire were intelligent children, and they were charming and resourceful, and had pleasant facial features, but they were extremely unlucky, and most everything that happened to them was rife with misfortune, misery and despair. I'm sorry to tell you this, but that's how the story goes."

From there, the morose narrator of *The Bad Beginning* explains how the Baudelaire children lost their parents in a fire that also destroyed their mansion home. The kids are then sent to live with Count Olaf, who claims to be their uncle. But it soon becomes clear that Count Olaf only wants the children's inheritance, which they cannot claim until they reach adulthood. As the tale progresses, he plots to seize the fortune by forcing 14-year-old Violet to marry him. But the Baudelaire children fight his dastardly plan. Armed with Violet's inventive mind, Klaus's uncanny skill at finding useful information in libraries, and baby Sunny's unusually sharp teeth, the bright and resourceful children foil his scheme and flee. Olaf promptly gives chase, setting the stage for subsequent volumes in the series.

The Bad Beginning received warm praise from critics. *Booklist,* for example, admitted that the author's "droll humor, reminiscent of Edward Gorey's, will be lost on some children." But the review added that "plenty of children will laugh at the over-the-top satire; hiss at the creepy nefarious villains; and root for the intelligent, courageous, unfortunate Baudelaire orphans."

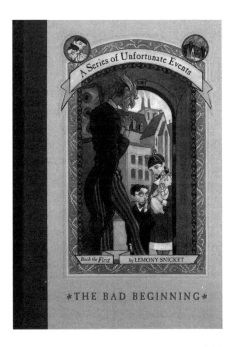

THE BAD BEGINNING

Soon the second and third books in *A Series of Unfortunate Events* were being whisked off store shelves by eager young readers. As with the opening book of the series, these books — *The Reptile Room* and *The Wide Window* — found the Baudelaire children in perpetual danger from the villainous Count Olaf, who turns out to be a master of disguise. In *The Reptile Room* (1999), the Baudelaire children are sent to live with their Uncle Monty, but Count Olaf arrives and devises a scheme to use their uncle's large reptile collection to capture the inheritance. In *The Wide Window* (2000), Violet and her brothers move in with their elderly Aunt Josephine, where they are joined by a sailboat captain who turns out to be Count Olaf.

As in the first book of the series, Snicket began both of these titles with an author's dedication to someone named "Beatrice," a mysterious love who has apparently died, to Snicket's everlasting sorrow. He also closed each book with a "cliffhanger"—a situation in which the Baudelaire children seem to be on the verge of death or capture by the evil Count.

As these books were released, publicity for Snicket's *Unfortunate Events* series grew by leaps and bounds. Children rushed out to buy each new book in the series, and critics applauded the author's ability to capture young readers' imaginations. *School Library Journal*, for example, stated that "the misfortunes [in the books] hover on the edge of being ridiculous, [but] Snicket's energetic blend of humor, dramatic irony, and literary flair makes it all perfectly believable." Other reviewers stated that Snicket managed to create suspense without truly frightening children. "Readers never truly worry that [the Baudelaire] orphans will be defeated in this or their next adventure," according to *Booklist.* Mystery writer Ayelet Waldman added that "Daniel gets it that children like to be scared. He also knows when to stop."

Snicket's Line of Bestsellers

In 2000 Snicket continued to release new books in the *Unfortunate Events* series. In the fourth book, *The Miserable Mill,* the Baudelaires are sent to a faraway town to live with a guardian who owns the Lucky Smells Lumbermill. But their lives are soon threatened once again by the vile Count Olaf. *Booklist* praised this fourth installment as "delicious" and "another plum for the orphans' fans." *The Austere Academy,* the fifth book in the series, finds the children enrolled at Prufrock Prep School, where they are forced to live in a shack and endure all sorts of terrible trials at the hands of instructors, students, and — of course — Count Olaf.

Snicket added three more books to *A Series of Unfortunate Events* in 2001. In *The Ersatz Elevator,* the Baudelaire kids go to live in a fancy penthouse apartment, but they are soon forced to put their own lives at risk to save two friends from Count Olaf's terrible clutches. This book prompted *School Library Journal* to note that "despite Snicket's perpetual caveats [warnings] to 'put this book down and pick up another one,' the Baudelaires are dynamic characters who inspire loyalty to the inevitable end of the series." In the

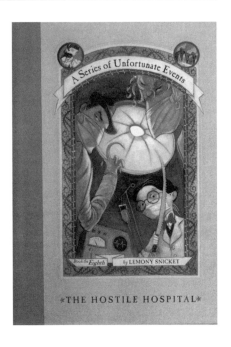

⋆THE HOSTILE HOSPITAL⋆

series' seventh book, *The Vile Village,* the children are sent to a terrible, crow-infested village that adopts orphans so that they can take care of all the town's unpleasant chores. And in *The Hostile Hospital,* Count Olaf disguises himself as a surgeon as part of an evil plan to cut off Violet's head during an operation.

All of these books were snapped up by children. Young readers loved following the adventures of the Baudelaire children, and they enjoyed Lemony Snicket's weird but engaging storytelling voice. In fact, by May 2002 seven of the eight titles from *A Series of Unfortunate Events* were on the Children's Bestseller List in the *New York Times.* Kids also flocked to the Lemony Snicket web site (www.lemonysnicket.com), where his unique brand of droll humor is on full display.

In recognition of the rising popularity of the Snicket books, Nickelodeon bought film and television rights to *A Series of Unfortunate Events.* In 2002 it was announced that Barry Sonnefeld, director of the *Men in Black* and *The Addams Family* movies, had signed a contract to direct the film version of the series. Sonnefeld's involvement delighted Snicket, who had agreed to write a screenplay for the movie.

In some ways, Snicket remains stunned by the popularity of the series. "[The reception for the series has] literally been beyond my wildest dreams," he said. "It's been an amazing and delightful sort of success be-

Lemony Snicket

cause I feel I'm doing good work. . . . The satisfying thing about writing for children is you never love a book the way you do when you are 10. To be in that place in a reader's head is almost a sacred experience."

Writing About Evil in a Scary World

The Lemony Snicket series has attracted strong support from many reviewers and fellow writers of books for children and young adults. Diane Roback, children's editor at *Publishers Weekly*, stated that "once in a great while a book comes along that feels completely fresh, and Lemony Snicket is it. [The series is] really antithetical to what most people think of as traditional kids' books—in fact, they take that whole gooey, smiley, happy-ending notion of children's literature and turn it right on its ear." Children's book writer Liz Rosenberg has commented that "I don't know when I've last seen a more original, funny, and eccentric group of books." And *Horn Book Magazine* reviewer Christine Heppermann notes that "Amidst all the irreverence in *A Series of Unfortunate Events* lie some genuinely poignant observations on perils more common to the average reader than swarms of ravenous leeches or imprisonment in towers. . . . *Unfortunate Events* acknowledges that not everything that happens in life is within one's control, especially if one is a child."

But the series has also been criticized by some adult readers. They feel that the books are excessively sad and scary and that they portray all adults as either evil, cowardly, or foolish. The Lemony Snicket books have also been condemned for dwelling too much on death, which is a concept that some of his younger readers do not completely understand. Concerns about the gloomy tone of *A Series of Unfortunate Events* were raised again after September 11, 2001, when terrorists slammed hijacked airplanes into New York's World Trade Center towers, the Pentagon in Washington, D.C., and Pennsylvania, killing thousands of people.

"[When] children write to me asking if Count Olaf is a terrorist, if the Baudelaires were anywhere near the World Trade Center, if the unnamed country where the books are set is in danger of being bombed, it is clear they are struggling with the same issues as the rest of us. . . . Certainly there are times when we want to escape to a trouble-free, imaginary world. But when the real world is so searing that it cannot be glossed over, we can find value in stories that admit the world is tumultuous, instead of reassuring us it is not."

Handler strongly defends the style and tone of his novels, though. "Since September 11, interviewers have asked me if it is appropriate to tell such stories, when there are plenty of real orphans and villains to worry about," he wrote in an article for the *New York Times*. "The answer, judging from the hundreds of e-mail messages and letters I have received, is that it is more than appropriate; it is necessary. My young readers are not only finding a

153

diversion in the melodrama of the Baudelaires' lives, but they are also finding ways of contemplating our current troubles through stories. The secret passageways, sinister reptiles, and nefarious disguises in my books may seem a far cry from the real world, but when children write to me asking if Count Olaf is a terrorist, if the Baudelaires were anywhere near the World Trade Center, if the unnamed country where the books are set is in danger of being bombed, it is clear they are struggling with the same issues as the rest of us. . . . Certainly there are times when we want to escape to a trouble-free, imaginary world. But when the real world is so searing that it cannot be glossed over, we can find value in stories that admit the world is tumultuous, instead of reassuring us it is not."

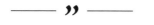

> *Snicket believes that by discussing evil in a comic way he makes it easier for young readers to "think about it more seriously and in a more complicated fashion. As the books go on, the children are forced to do more and more things that they're uncomfortable doing in order to escape from evil, and they worry a lot as they find themselves doing things like donning disguises or hiding or running away from authority figures. They worry about themselves becoming evil, and I think that's a very serious issue and something that's not often explored in books for children."*

Snicket also believes that by discussing evil in a comic way he makes it easier for young readers to "think about it more seriously and in a more complicated fashion. As the books go on, the children are forced to do more and more things that they're uncomfortable doing in order to escape from evil, and they worry a lot as they find themselves doing things like donning disguises or hiding or running away from authority figures. They worry about themselves becoming evil, and I think that's a very serious issue and something that's not often explored in books for children. There's usually a very clear bad guy and a very clear good guy. And in [my books], although there is a very clear bad guy, there begins to be sort of murky circumstances under how much of a bad guy are you willing to become in order to defeat a bad guy. And that, to me, seems a terribly relevant issue now. It's not something that I want to shy away from after the attacks on the 11th."

The mysterious Lemony Snicket wrote an autobiography, whose book jacket looks like a plain brown wrapper (left). But on the reverse side is a fake jacket, which can be used to disguise the book (right). Then, to further compound the mystery, the actual book cover features a photo of the secretive Snicket and a false obituary notice (see also page 156).

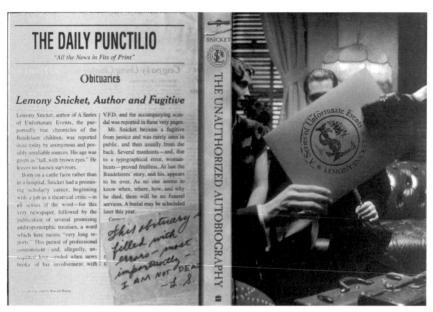

The actual cover of Snicket's autobiography, with his photo and the false obituary notice (see also page 155).

The "Secret" Identity of Lemony Snicket

In 2002 the author continued to have great fun with his Lemony Snicket character. In the spring he released *Lemony Snicket: The Unauthorized Autobiography,* a book full of codes, riddles, photographs, and other clues about the identity and background of the series' strange narrator. In reality, the riddles and photographs only deepen the mystery surrounding the Snicket character, but reviewers praised it as an amusing diversion for fans of the *Unfortunate Events* series. "A certain maniacal glee went into the creation of this archly humorous volume," said *Publishers Weekly*. "The contents lead readers on a merry goose chase. . . . Readers are left as nearly in the dark about Snicket as they were at the start. Of course, this is all part of the fun, guaranteed to make the author's fans itch to get their hands on a copy of this devious romp masquerading as an autobiography."

When making personal appearances at schools and bookstores, the author pretends that Lemony Snicket is a real person. At each appearance, he introduces himself as "Mr. Snicket's personal representative" and explains that Snicket will not be appearing because he has been injured in a strange accident or a weird encounter with a shark or other fearsome creature. At most appearances, the children in the audience laugh and shout at this news, for they know that Handler is really Snicket.

Snicket then proceeds to entertain his young audience with songs, readings from the *Unfortunate Events* books, and humorous descriptions of the unfortunate Snicket. "[He] is an astonishingly gifted performer," wrote Daphne Merkin in the *New York Times Magazine* after one appearance. "Forty- five minutes into his act . . . the crowd of kids and teachers and bookstore staff is still captivated. He is reading from *The Bad Beginning,* encouraging the kids to come in with sound effects. . . . Then he whisks out an accordion and accompanies himself as he sings [a song called] 'Scream and Run Away.'" Merkin also noted with approval that when he signs books for children, "he takes a lot of time with each child, especially the tentative ones, perversely urging them to save their money and not buy the books or, if they insist on doing so, to bury them in the yard when they get home, or burn them in the fireplace, or coat them in tuna and feed them to the cat. Anything but read them, in other words. The kids look puzzled but delighted, which is exactly the sort of response Handler wants."

Snicket has announced that A *Series of Unfortunate Events* will be a 13-book series. During the first couple years of the series, he released two or three books a year. But beginning with the ninth installment — *The Carnivorous Carnival,* due in October 2002 — he intends to publish only one book a year. "It was really hard to make that decision," he admits. "I have a very clear memory that as a kid I would go to the library once a week to look for books by Zilpha Keatley Snyder, who wrote pretty quickly, but never quickly enough for me. . . . It's hard when kids ask when the next book is coming out. You want the answer to be 'Oh, well, it's right here!' So to say next year is a bummer, but it also feels good to sleep, which I wasn't doing for a while."

> *"[He] is an astonishingly gifted performer," wrote Daphne Merkin in the* **New York Times Magazine** *after one appearance before an audience of kids and adults. "Forty-five minutes into his act . . . the crowd of kids and teachers and bookstore staff is still captivated. He is reading from* **The Bad Beginning,** *encouraging the kids to come in with sound effects. . . . Then he whisks out an accordion and accompanies himself as he sings [a song called] 'Scream and Run Away.'"*

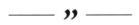

MARRIAGE AND FAMILY

Daniel Handler married Lisa Brown, a graphic artist and illustrator, in 1998. They have no children.

HOBBIES AND OTHER INTERESTS

Snicket enjoys classical music, and he is a talented accordion player. "I took up the accordion in college because I wanted to drive my parents crazy," he recalled. He also helped write songs that appear at the end of each audio recording of the *Unfortunate Events* series. Other hobbies that he enjoys include cooking and reading.

WRITINGS

A Series of Unfortunate Events (writing as Lemony Snicket)

The Bad Beginning, 1999
The Reptile Room, 1999
The Wide Window, 2000
The Miserable Mill, 2000
The Austere Academy, 2000
The Ersatz Elevator, 2001
The Vile Village, 2001
The Hostile Hospital, 2001
A Series of Unfortunate Events (collection containing *The Bad Beginning, The Reptile Room,* and *The Wide Window*), 2001

Lemony Snicket: The Unauthorized Autobiography, 2002 (writing as Lemony Snicket)

Adult Fiction (writing as Daniel Handler)

The Basic Eight, 1999
Watch Your Mouth, 2000

HONORS AND AWARDS

Academy of American Poets Prize: 1990
Olin Fellowship: 1992

FURTHER READING

Books

Something About the Author, Vol. 126, 2002

Periodicals

ALAN Review, Winter 2001, p.35

Book, July 2001, p.81

Booklist, Mar. 15, 1999, p.1289; Dec. 1, 1999, p.707; May 1, 2000, p.1670;
   Oct. 15, 2000, p.439

Boston Globe, May 19, 2002, p.E5

Christian Science Monitor, Aug. 12, 1999, p.21

Dallas Morning News, Feb. 17, 2002, p.C1

Entertainment Weekly, May 24, 2002, p.56; June 7, 2002, p.67

Horn Book Magazine, Mar. 2001, p.239

Los Angeles Times, Sep. 9, 2001, p.E1

Maclean's, Dec. 18, 2000, p.84

New York Times, Oct. 30, 2001, p.A17

New York Times Magazine, Apr. 29, 2001, p.62

Newsweek, June 24, 2002, p.95

People Weekly, May 27, 2002, p.155

Philadelphia Inquirer, May 19, 2002, p.H1

Publishers Weekly, Sep. 6, 1999, p.104; Jan. 17, 2000, p.58; May 29, 2000,
   p.42; May 6, 2002, p.59

San Francisco Chronicle, May 26, 2002, p.D1

School Library Journal, Nov. 1999, p.165; July 2000, p.110; Oct. 2000, p.171;
   Aug. 2001, p.188

U.S. News and World Report, May 20, 2002, p.10

Online Articles

http://www.kidsreads.com/features/010314-lemony-snicket.asp
   (*KidsReads.com,* "A Series of Unfortunate Events," undated)

http://www.nancymatson.com/authorinterviews/snicket.htm
   (*Nancy Matson's Web Site,* "Children's Author Interview — Lemony
   Snicket," Mar. 2000)

http://www.timeforkids.com/TFK/explore/story/0,6079,249604,00.html
   (*TimeForKids.com,* "Lemony Snicket, Author," undated)

Online Database

Biography Resource Center, 2002, article from *Contemporary Authors Online,*
   2001

Other

"Fresh Air," National Public Radio (NPR) transcript, Dec. 10, 2001

ADDRESS

HarperCollins Children's Books
1350 Avenue of the Americas
New York, NY 10019

e-mail: lsnicket@harpercollins.com

WORLD WIDE WEB SITE

http://www.lemonysnicket.com

Photo and Illustration Credits

An Na/Photos: Front Street Books; courtesy of the author, An Na. Cover: A STEP FROM HEAVEN Front Street Books.

Claude Brown/Photos: AP/Wide World Photos; LeRoy McLucas (page 25); copyright © Bettmann/ CORBIS. Covers: MANCHILD IN THE PROMISED LAND Macmillan Publishing Co., Inc. Copyright © Claude Brown 1965 (hardbound); Touchstone Books/ A Simon & Schuster Trade Paperback.

Meg Cabot/Photo: Reven Wurman. Covers: ALL-AMERICAN GIRL, THE PRINCESS DIARIES, and PRINCESS IN LOVE all HarperCollins Publishers; SHADOWLAND Simon Pulse/An imprint of Simon & Schuster; NICOLA AND THE VISCOUNT Avon Paperback.

Virginia Hamilton/Covers: BLUISH; HER STORIES; A RING OF TRICKSTERS; SEC- OND COUSINS and WHEN BIRDS COULD TALK AND BATS COULD SING all Scholastic; THE HOUSE OF DIES DREAR; M.C. HIGGINS, THE GREAT; THE PLANET OF JUNIOR BROWN and ZEELY all Aladdin Paperbacks; THE GIRL WHO SPUN GOLD Blue Sky Press/Scholastic; THE PEOPLE COULD FLY by Virginia Hamilton. Cover art copyright © 1985 by Leo and Diane Dillon and MANY THOU- SAND GONE by Virginia Hamilton. Cover art copyright © 1993 by Leo and Diane Dillon. Both reprinted by permission of Alfred A. Knopf, Inc., a subsidiary of Random House, Inc.; SWEET WHISPERS, BROTHER RUSH HarperTrophy, a division of HarperCollins Publishers; ANTHONY BURNS Dell courtesy of Laurel-Leaf Books, an imprint of Random House Children's Books, a division of Random House, Inc.

Chuck Jones/Photos: AP/Wide World Photos; copyright © Warner Bros./Photofest; *The Phantom Tollbooth* copyright © 1972 Metro-Goldwyn-Mayer, Inc.

Robert Lipsyte/Photo: Courtesy of The New York Times Company. Covers: THE BRAVE; THE CONTENDER and ONE FAT SUMMER all HarperTrophy, a division of HarperCollins Publishers; THE CHEMO KID; FREE TO BE MUHAMMAD ALI and MICHAEL JORDAN all HarperCollins Publishers; NIGGER Washington Square Press/A Simon & Schuster Trade Paperback.

Lillian Morrison/Photo: Copyright © Will & Deni McIntyre/CORBIS. Covers: I SCREAM, YOU SCREAM copyright © 1997 by Lillian Morrison, courtesy August House Pub- lishers; MORE SPICE THAN SUGAR Houghton Mifflin Company; WAY TO GO! text copyright © 2001 by Lillian Morrison. Illustrations copyright © by Susan Spellman, courtesy Boyds Mills Press; YOURS TILL NIAGARA FALLS Thomas Y. Crowell Company.

PHOTO AND ILLUSTRATION CREDITS

Linda Sue Park/Photo: Klaus Pollmeier. Covers: A SINGLE SHARD and WHEN MY NAME WAS KEOKO both Clarion Books; THE KITE FIGHTERS and SEESAW GIRL both courtesy of Dell Yearling, an imprint of Random House Children's Books, a division of Random House, Inc.

Pam Muñoz Ryan/Covers: ESPERANZA RISING; RIDING FREEDOM and WHEN MARIAN SANG all Scholastic.

Lemony Snicket/Photo: Steve Labadessa/PEOPLE Weekly; Meredith Heuer; Lemony Snicket captured on film by Meredith Heuer. Covers: A SERIES OF UNFORTUNATE EVENTS: THE BAD BEGINNING and THE HOSTILE HOSPITAL and THE MISERABLE MILL all Harper Trophy, a division of HarperCollins Publishers; LEMONY SNICKET: THE UNAUTHORIZED AUTOBIOGRAPHY HarperCollins Publishers.

How to Use the Cumulative Index

Our indexes have a new look. In an effort to make our indexes easier to use, we've combined the Name and General Index into a new, Cumulative Index. This single ready-reference resource covers all the volumes in *Biography Today,* both the general series and the special subject series. The new Cumulative Index contains complete listings of all individuals who have appeared in *Biography Today* since the series began. Their names appear in bold-faced type, followed by the issue in which they appear. The Cumulative Index also includes references for the occupations, nationalities, and ethnic and minority origins of individuals profiled in *Biography Today.*

We have also made some changes to our specialty indexes, the Places of Birth Index and the Birthday Index. To consolidate and to save space, the Places of Birth Index and the Birthday Index will no longer appear in the January and April issues of the softbound subscription series. But these indexes can still be found in the September issue of the softbound subscription series, in the hardbound Annual Cumulation at the end of each year, and in each volume of the special subject series.

General Series

The General Series of *Biography Today* is denoted in the index with the month and year of the issue in which the individual appeared. Each individual also appears in the Annual Cumulation for that year.

Special Subject Series

The Special Subject Series of *Biography Today* are each denoted in the index with an abbreviated form of the series name, plus the number of the volume in which the individual appears. They are listed as follows.

Adams, Ansel	Artist V.1	(Artists Series)
Cabot, Meg.	Author V.12	(Author Series)
Fauci, Anthony	Science V.7	(Scientists & Inventors Series)
Iverson, Allen.	Sport V.7	(Sports Series)
Peterson, Roger Tory	WorLdr V.1	(World Leaders Series: Environmental Leaders)
Sadat, Anwar	WorLdr V.2	(World Leaders Series: Modern African Leaders)
Wolf, Hazel.	WorLdr V.3	(World Leaders Series: Environmental Leaders 2)

Updates

Updated information on selected individuals appears in the Appendix at the end of the *Biography Today* Annual Cumulation. In the index, the original entry is listed first, followed by any updates.

Arafat, Yasir . . . . Sep 94; Update 94;
    Update 95; Update 96; Update 97; Update 98;
    Update 00; Update 01
Gates, Bill . . . . Apr 93; Update 98;
    Update 00; Science V.5; Update 01
Griffith Joyner, Florence. . . . . Sport V.1;
    Update 98
Sanders, Barry . . . . Sep 95; Update 99
Spock, Dr. Benjamin . . . . Sep 95; Update 98
Yeltsin, Boris . . . . Apr 92; Update 93;
    Update 95; Update 96; Update 98; Update 00

Cumulative Index

This cumulative index includes names, occupations, nationalities, and ethnic and minority origins that pertain to all individuals profiled in *Biography Today* since the debut of the series in 1992.

193

Places of Birth Index

The following index lists the places of birth for the individuals profiled in *Biography Today*. Places of birth are entered under state, province, and/or country.

203

205

Birthday Index

July (continued)	Year
6 Bush, George W.	1946
Dalai Lama	1935
Dumitriu, Ioana	1976
7 Chagall, Marc	1887
Heinlein, Robert	1907
Kwan, Michelle	1980
Sakic, Joe	1969
Stachowski, Richie	1985
8 Hardaway, Anfernee "Penny"	1971
Sealfon, Rebecca	1983
9 Farmer, Nancy	1941
Hanks, Tom	1956
Hassan II	1929
Krim, Mathilde	1926
Sacks, Oliver	1933
10 Ashe, Arthur	1943
Boulmerka, Hassiba	1969
11 Cisneros, Henry	1947
White, E.B.	1899
12 Bauer, Joan	1951
Cosby, Bill	1937
Johnson, Johanna	1983
Yamaguchi, Kristi	1972
13 Ford, Harrison	1942
Stewart, Patrick	1940
15 Aristide, Jean-Bertrand	1953
Ventura, Jesse	1951
16 Johnson, Jimmy	1943
Sanders, Barry	1968
17 An Na	1972
Stepanek, Mattie	1990
18 Glenn, John	1921
Lemelson, Jerome	1923
Mandela, Nelson	1918
19 Tarvin, Herbert	1985
20 Hillary, Sir Edmund	1919
21 Chastain, Brandi	1968
Reno, Janet	1938
Riley, Dawn	1964
Williams, Robin	1952
22 Calder, Alexander	1898
Dole, Bob	1923
Hinton, S.E.	1948
23 Haile Selassie	1892
Williams, Michelle	1980
24 Abzug, Bella	1920
Krone, Julie	1963
Lopez, Jennifer	1970
Moss, Cynthia	1940
Wilson, Mara	1987

	Year
25 Payton, Walter	1954
26 Berenstain, Jan	1923
27 Dunlap, Alison	1969
Rodriguez, Alex	1975
28 Davis, Jim	1945
Pottter, Beatrix	1866
29 Burns, Ken	1953
Creech, Sharon	1945
Dole, Elizabeth Hanford	1936
Jennings, Peter	1938
Morris, Wanya	1973
30 Hill, Anita	1956
Moore, Henry	1898
Schroeder, Pat	1940
31 Cronin, John	1950
Radcliffe, Daniel	1989
Reid Banks, Lynne	1929
Rowling, J. K.	1965
Weinke, Chris	1972

August	Year
1 Brown, Ron	1941
Coolio	1963
Garcia, Jerry	1942
2 Baldwin, James	1924
Healy, Bernadine	1944
3 Brady, Tom	1977
Roper, Dee Dee	?
Savimbi, Jonas	1934
4 Gordon, Jeff	1971
5 Córdova, France	1947
Ewing, Patrick	1962
Jackson, Shirley Ann	1946
6 Cooney, Barbara	1917
Robinson, David	1965
Warhol, Andy	?1928
7 Byars, Betsy	1928
Duchovny, David	1960
Leakey, Louis	1903
Villa-Komaroff, Lydia	1947
8 Boyd, Candy Dawson	1946
Chasez, JC	1976
9 Anderson, Gillian	1968
Holdsclaw, Chamique	1977
Houston, Whitney	1963
McKissack, Patricia C.	1944
Sanders, Deion	1967
Travers, P.L.	?1899
11 Haley, Alex	1921
Hogan, Hulk	1953
Rowan, Carl T.	1925
Wozniak, Steve	1950

Biography Today

Subject Series

Expands and complements the General Series and targets specific subject areas ...

Our readers asked for it! They wanted more biographies, and the *Biography Today* Subject Series is our response to that demand. Now your readers can choose their special areas of interest and go on to read about their favorites in those fields. Priced at just $39 per volume, the following specific volumes are included in the *Biography Today* Subject Series:

- **Artists Series**
- **Author Series**
- **Scientists & Inventors Series**
- **Sports Series**
- **World Leaders Series**
  Environmental Leaders
  Modern African Leaders

FEATURES AND FORMAT

- Sturdy 6" x 9" hardbound volumes
- Individual volumes, $39 each
- 200 pages per volume
- 10-12 profiles per volume — targets individuals within a specific subject area
- Contact sources for additional information
- Cumulative General, Places of Birth, and Birthday Indexes

NOTE: There is *no duplication of entries* between the **General Series** of *Biography Today* and the **Subject Series**.

AUTHOR SERIES

"A useful tool for children's assignment needs." — *School Library Journal*

"The prose is workmanlike: report writers will find enough detail to begin sound investigations, and browsers are likely to find someone of interest." — *School Library Journal*

SCIENTISTS & INVENTORS SERIES

"The articles are readable, attractively laid out, and touch on important points that will suit assignment needs. Browsers will note the clear writing and interesting details." — *School Library Journal*

"The book is excellent for demonstrating that scientists are real people with widely diverse backgrounds and personal interests. The biographies are fascinating to read." — *The Science Teacher*

SPORTS SERIES

"This series should become a standard resource in libraries that serve intermediate students." — *School Library Journal*

ENVIRONMENTAL LEADERS #1

"A tremendous book that fills a gap in the biographical category of books. This is a great reference book." — *Science Scope*

Artists Series

VOLUME 1

Ansel Adams
Romare Bearden
Margaret Bourke-White
Alexander Calder
Marc Chagall
Helen Frankenthaler
Jasper Johns
Jacob Lawrence
Henry Moore
Grandma Moses
Louise Nevelson
Georgia O'Keeffe
Gordon Parks
I.M. Pei
Diego Rivera
Norman Rockwell
Andy Warhol
Frank Lloyd Wright

Author Series

VOLUME 1

Eric Carle
Alice Childress
Robert Cormier
Roald Dahl
Jim Davis
John Grisham
Virginia Hamilton
James Herriot
S.E. Hinton
M.E. Kerr
Stephen King
Gary Larson
Joan Lowery Nixon
Gary Paulsen
Cynthia Rylant
Mildred D. Taylor
Kurt Vonnegut, Jr.
E.B. White
Paul Zindel

VOLUME 2

James Baldwin
Stan and Jan Berenstain
David Macaulay
Patricia MacLachlan

Scott O'Dell
Jerry Pinkney
Jack Prelutsky
Lynn Reid Banks
Faith Ringgold
J.D. Salinger
Charles Schulz
Maurice Sendak
P.L. Travers
Garth Williams

VOLUME 3

Candy Dawson Boyd
Ray Bradbury
Gwendolyn Brooks
Ralph W. Ellison
Louise Fitzhugh
Jean Craighead George
E.L. Konigsburg
C.S. Lewis
Fredrick L. McKissack
Patricia C. McKissack
Katherine Paterson
Anne Rice
Shel Silverstein
Laura Ingalls Wilder

VOLUME 4

Betsy Byars
Chris Carter
Caroline B. Cooney
Christopher Paul Curtis
Anne Frank
Robert Heinlein
Marguerite Henry
Lois Lowry
Melissa Mathison
Bill Peet
August Wilson

VOLUME 5

Sharon Creech
Michael Crichton
Karen Cushman
Tomie dePaola
Lorraine Hansberry
Karen Hesse
Brian Jacques
Gary Soto
Richard Wright
Laurence Yep

VOLUME 6

Lloyd Alexander
Paula Danziger
Nancy Farmer
Zora Neale Hurston
Shirley Jackson
Angela Johnson
Jon Krakauer
Leo Lionni
Francine Pascal
Louis Sachar
Kevin Williamson

VOLUME 7

William H. Armstrong
Patricia Reilly Giff
Langston Hughes
Stan Lee
Julius Lester
Robert Pinsky
Todd Strasser
Jacqueline Woodson
Patricia C. Wrede
Jane Yolen

VOLUME 8

Amelia Atwater-Rhodes
Barbara Cooney
Paul Laurence Dunbar
Ursula K. Le Guin
Farley Mowat
Naomi Shihab Nye
Daniel Pinkwater
Beatrix Potter
Ann Rinaldi

VOLUME 9

Robb Armstrong
Cherie Bennett
Bruce Coville
Rosa Guy
Harper Lee
Irene Gut Opdyke
Philip Pullman
Jon Scieszka
Amy Tan
Joss Whedon

VOLUME 10

David Almond
Joan Bauer
Kate DiCamillo
Jack Gantos
Aaron McGruder
Richard Peck

Andrea Davis Pinkney
Louise Rennison
David Small
Katie Tarbox

VOLUME 11

Laurie Halse Anderson
Bryan Collier
Margaret Peterson
   Haddix
Milton Meltzer
William Sleator
Sonya Sones
Genndy Tartakovsky
Wendelin Van Draanen
Ruth White

VOLUME 12

An Na
Claude Brown
Meg Cabot
Virginia Hamilton
Chuck Jones
Robert Lipsyte
Lillian Morrison
Linda Sue Park
Pam Muñoz Ryan
Lemony Snicket
   (Daniel Handler)

Scientists & Inventors Series

VOLUME 1

John Bardeen
Sylvia Earle
Dian Fossey
Jane Goodall
Bernadine Healy
Jack Horner
Mathilde Krim
Edwin Land
Louise & Mary Leakey
Rita Levi-Montalcini
J. Robert Oppenheimer
Albert Sabin
Carl Sagan
James D. Watson

VOLUME 2

Jane Brody
Seymour Cray
Paul Erdös
Walter Gilbert
Stephen Jay Gould
Shirley Ann Jackson
Raymond Kurzweil
Shannon Lucid
Margaret Mead
Garrett Morgan
Bill Nye
Eloy Rodriguez
An Wang

VOLUME 3

Luis W. Alvarez
Hans A. Bethe
Gro Harlem Brundtland
Mary S. Calderone
Ioana Dumitriu
Temple Grandin
John Langston
   Gwaltney
Bernard Harris
Jerome Lemelson
Susan Love
Ruth Patrick
Oliver Sacks
Richie Stachowski

VOLUME 4

David Attenborough
Robert Ballard
Ben Carson
Eileen Collins
Biruté Galdikas
Lonnie Johnson
Meg Lowman
Forrest Mars Sr.
Akio Morita
Janese Swanson

VOLUME 5

Steve Case
Douglas Engelbart
Shawn Fanning
Sarah Flannery
Bill Gates
Laura Groppe
Grace Murray Hopper
Steven Jobs
Rand and Robyn Miller
Shigeru Miyamoto
Steve Wozniak

VOLUME 6

Hazel Barton
Alexa Canady
Arthur Caplan
Francis Collins
Gertrude Elion
Henry Heimlich
David Ho
Kenneth Kamler
Lucy Spelman
Lydia Villa-Komaroff

VOLUME 7

Tim Berners-Lee
France Córdova
Anthony S. Fauci
Sue Hendrickson
Steve Irwin
John Forbes Nash, Jr.
Jerri Nielsen
Ryan Patterson
Nina Vasan
Gloria WilderBrathwaite

Sports Series

VOLUME 1

Hank Aaron
Kareem Abdul-Jabbar
Hassiba Boulmerka
Susan Butcher
Beth Daniel
Chris Evert
Ken Griffey, Jr.
Florence Griffith Joyner
Grant Hill
Greg LeMond
Pelé
Uta Pippig
Cal Ripken, Jr.
Arantxa Sanchez Vicario
Deion Sanders
Tiger Woods

VOLUME 2

Muhammad Ali
Donovan Bailey
Gail Devers
John Elway
Brett Favre
Mia Hamm
Anfernee "Penny"
   Hardaway
Martina Hingis
Gordie Howe
Jack Nicklaus
Richard Petty
Dot Richardson
Sheryl Swoopes
Steve Yzerman

VOLUME 3

Joe Dumars
Jim Harbaugh
Dominik Hasek
Michelle Kwan
Rebecca Lobo
Greg Maddux
Fatuma Roba
Jackie Robinson
John Stockton
Picabo Street
Pat Summitt
Amy Van Dyken

VOLUME 4

Wilt Chamberlain
Brandi Chastain
Derek Jeter
Karch Kiraly
Alex Lowe
Randy Moss
Se Ri Pak
Dawn Riley
Karen Smyers
Kurt Warner
Serena Williams

VOLUME 5

Vince Carter
Lindsay Davenport
Lisa Fernandez
Fu Mingxia
Jaromir Jagr
Marion Jones
Pedro Martinez
Warren Sapp
Jenny Thompson
Karrie Webb

VOLUME 6

Jennifer Capriati
Stacy Dragila
Kevin Garnett
Eddie George
Alex Rodriguez
Joe Sakic
Annika Sorenstam
Jackie Stiles
Tiger Woods
Aliy Zirkle

VOLUME 7

Tom Brady
Tara Dakides
Alison Dunlap
Sergio Garcia
Allen Iverson
Shirley Muldowney
Ty Murray
Patrick Roy
Tasha Schwikert

World Leaders Series

VOLUME 1: Environmental Leaders 1

Edward Abbey
Renee Askins
David Brower
Rachel Carson
Marjory Stoneman
   Douglas
Dave Foreman
Lois Gibbs
Wangari Maathai
Chico Mendes
Russell A. Mittermeier
Margaret and Olaus J.
   Murie
Patsy Ruth Oliver
Roger Tory Peterson
Ken Saro-Wiwa
Paul Watson
Adam Werbach

VOLUME 2:
Modern African
Leaders

Mohammed Farah
    Aidid
Idi Amin
Hastings Kamuzu Banda
Haile Selassie
Hassan II
Kenneth Kaunda
Jomo Kenyatta
Winnie Mandela
Mobutu Sese Seko
Robert Mugabe
Kwame Nkrumah
Julius Kambarage
    Nyerere
Anwar Sadat
Jonas Savimbi
Léopold Sédar Senghor
William V. S. Tubman

VOLUME 3:
Environmental
Leaders 2

John Cronin
Dai Qing
Ka Hsaw Wa
Winona LaDuke
Aldo Leopold
Bernard Martin
Cynthia Moss
John Muir
Gaylord Nelson
Douglas Tompkins
Hazel Wolf